Praise for

The Wisdom Seeker

"This book will shock, amaze and inspire you…all at the same time! Pisey Leng survived the killing fields of Cambodia, another nine years of fighting for her life and her freedom only to learn that her greatest enemy was herself. The Wisdom Seeker will show you how to use your mind's power to triumph over any adversity and enjoy all the riches you desire."
—Bob Proctor, Star of the movie *The Secret*, Best-Selling Author, World Leader in Personal Development

The Wisdom Seeker is a genuine triumph of humanity. A courageous and dramatic story, and the author/survivor shares her struggles when finally set free from the horrific killing fields of Cambodia. Pisey teaches us that no matter what you are faced with, it is choice to forgive, be grateful and find happiness in the midst of great tragedy. She is an inspirational lady with an amazing story. I highly recommend this to everyone."
—Peggy McColl, New York Times Best-Selling Author, aka "The Best-Seller Maker",
http://peggymccoll.com

"Beautifully written with heartfelt honesty. Unlike most books on the killing fields of Cambodia, Pisey does not focus on the tragic, devastating details but rather one survivor's journey to happiness and serenity. The Wisdom Seeker has the capacity to take you on a journey you may have never walked before that will lead you to a path of self-realization in a new way. This book contains gifts that are timeless. We just have to let go of the bad things and embrace change for what it's worth. Life lessons are priceless."
—Judy O'Beirn,
International Best-Selling Author of *Unwavering Strength*

"A very personal first-hand account from a survivor of the Khmer Rouge, The Wisdom Seeker is engaging from the very first page. While Pisey Leng's journey was sad and tragic, she found her way through it with an amazing attitude and the exceptional desire to help others heal in their own lives. She shows us it's all about changing your perceptions and understanding that you alone have the power to let go and find what truly makes you happy."
—Brian Proctor, VP of Business Development, Proctor Gallagher Institute

"A fantastic read for anyone. My heart bleeds for those who suffered under the Khmer Rouge. Pisey Leng's experience was so horrible and yet so inspiring when I read of her survival, escape, and triumph to thriving. She takes you with her on her hero's journey and then

gives you the tools to overcome your own challenges, this book is truly engaging and historically informative. I highly recommend!"
—Karen Smith, www.findingpurpose.com

"*The Wisdom Seeker* is incredible story of finding the sunlight in an unimaginable dark situation. Pisey Leng is the ultimate example of how you can move forward from tremendous hardship and tragedy, and still use the amazing power you have within to create the life you desire."
—Casey Demchak, Award-winning Copywriter & Consultant

The Wisdom Seeker

Finding the Seed of Advantage in the Khmer Rouge

PISEY LENG
As told to Jennifer Colford

Foreword by Rob Hamill, Olympian
and #1 Best-Selling Author

Published by
Hasmark Publishing
1-888-402-0027 ext. 101

Copy Editor
Sigrid Macdonald
http://www.bookmagic.ca/

Cover Design
NZ Graphics
www.nzgraphics.com

Layout
Ginger Marks DocUmeant Designs
www.DocUmeantDesigns.com

ISBN-13: 978-0-9920116-3-5
ISBN-10: 0992011639

Dedication

To my mother, who has been a pillar of strength in my life, my savior, my guiding light, my inspiration. Thank you for your unconditional love and encouraging me to be the best that I can be.

To my father, whose love and guidance saved my life many times during my darkest days. Even though he was taken from my life in such a brutal way when I was still a very young girl, his love and guidance will live in my heart forever.

To my brother, for your love and caring nature that is evident to all who know you.

To my husband and my two sons, whose unconditional love and support help make the impossible possible.

I love you all.

Contents

Part Three

Foreword

"You need to speak with Pisey!"

Wise words from my friend, Mike, with whom I had just been discussing our family story, the film I was working on, and my impending appearance at Cambodia's war crimes tribunal, the Extraordinary Chambers in the Courts of Cambodia (ECCC). I was to testify against the first Khmer Rouge defendant charged with crimes against humanity, Comrade Duch: the commander who ran Tuol Sleng prison (code-named S21). The prison had been dubbed "the mother of all torture centers" in Cambodia, where the Comrade oversaw the interrogation and execution of at least 12,000 men, women, and children. One of those victims was my brother Kerry Hamill.

Now, thirty-one years later, I had embarked on a search for truth and forgiveness. Before this journey could take place,

I needed advice and, perhaps most importantly, support and endorsement from those who had survived the killing fields. As a Westerner who did not suffer directly under Pol Pot's brutal regime, I was in the unenviable position of representing my brother (and potentially all "foreigner" victims of the regime) but not necessarily Cambodian survivors. How would Cambodians respond to my quest? Would New Zealand's expat Cambodian community support me? Or would they damn me as a "barang" who should keep out of Cambodia's affairs?

Taking Mike's advice, I made Pisey the first person I spoke with, and she immediately put my mind at ease. After a brief telephone conversation, we had agreed we would meet "sometime over the next week or so." A few days later, I turned up unannounced at her fantastic café. Her warm smile and open manner made her feel like an old friend. After I introduced myself, Pisey hugged me and then took me aside to a table at the rear of the café where we talked about the Khmer Rouge, the atrocities, and the effects it all had on both our families. We held hands across the table, and together we wept.

We wept for our lost loved ones; we wept for all the Khmer Rouge victims and their families; and we wept for the perpetrators who had become so dehumanized that they performed incomprehensible acts of depravity. Then Pisey started to tell me her incredible story.

The empathy and depth of feeling Pisey exhibited that day allayed my fears. I would have understood if she had been angry and bitter, but her attitude was totally the opposite. Despite unbelievable pain, she exhibited a truly amazing, heartwarming spirit, which made me feel like family. She gave me the strength and reinforcement I needed. I realised that the person before me was an incredible human being, one who had the poise and humility to not only succeed on her life's journey but also to actively support others on theirs.

In reality, I knew relatively little of Pisey's story. Until now. *The Wisdom Seeker* is an incredible story of love, hope, perseverance and redemption. The way she dealt with unimaginable hardship, sadness, and challenges will fill you with a sense of awe. Pisey's story evokes so many emotions, not least that surrounding her mother—her rock, a formidable force whose work ethic, sense of timing, and ability to act on instinct is a revelation. Many times, Pisey's mother saved her children's lives. She was set up by jealous neighbors. That should have resulted in her execution, yet she responded without any resentment toward her conspiring "friends." That is utterly inspiring.

Patrons would never imagine the lovely, humble lady that is Pisey's mother, who now serves up her magic at the local café, had gone through such trauma saving the lives of her children along the way.

The Wisdom Seeker reminds me of Viktor Frankl's eminent Man's Search for Meaning. Frankl, an Auschwitz survivor, noted: "Forces beyond your control can take away everything you possess except one thing, your freedom to choose how you will respond to the situation."

Pisey and her family responded with incredible courage and determination. And throughout their collective struggle to freedom, they never lost hope.

For Pisey to finally regain her freedom only to meet her biggest foe–herself–and how she turned around perhaps the darkest moments of her life is where the biggest lessons for all can be taken.

Rob Hamill MNZM
Olympian, Trans-Atlantic rowing champion and motivational speaker
Author #1 Best-Seller *The Naked Rower*
Producer of award-winning documentary film *Brother Number One*
www.RobHamill.com

Acknowledgments

I would like to express my sincere gratitude to the following people who helped make my dream of this book a reality.

Jennifer Colford for her amazing skills, dedication, and total commitment to this project. Without her, this book would not be what it is now. The words "Thank You" just do not do justice for what she has done for me and for my book.

Peggy McColl for coaching me and making me believe that I could take on this project and make this book a reality. Her skills and guidance are incredible.

Rob Hamill for his support over the years. His life achievements and his pursuit for justice for his brother Kerry, who was tortured and murdered in S-21 by the Khmer Rouge, are very inspiring, exceptional, and heartwarming.

Guy De Smet for his encouragement and support for connecting me with Jennifer.

Bob Proctor for his teaching and mentoring that completely changed my life for the better. His Mastermind Summit was the catalyst for this project.

Judy O'Beirn, Jenn Gibson, and the team at Hasmark Services for their amazing professional service that turns the impossible into a miracle.

My family and friends in New Zealand and abroad for believing in me and supporting this project right through to the end.

Preface

Dear Reader,

I wrote this book to share my story and help others heal as I have. Through my search for wisdom, I have learned that there is a seed of advantage in every situation, and by seeking wisdom, peace, and happiness, I have been rewarded with an abundant life filled with love, joy, and serenity.

Surviving the killing fields is only part of my story. Like millions of Cambodians forced from my home in Phnom Penh into the countryside, I suffered like all so-called newcomers. My dad was executed, and my mom was nearly executed as a result of treachery in a story I will share with you in this book. My brother and I suffered from starvation and infections that left us scarred both mentally and physically. All the new-comers were terrorized and tortured, and we came very close to dying from exhaustion from the long hours of forced labor.

I experienced grueling living conditions where our family was forced to live in a tiny hut with another family from the city. There were no sanitary facilities, and we endured constant fear of punishment or death. This was during the best of times for my family living under the Khmer Rouge. I witnessed many horrific and gruesome events that I cannot erase from my memory, despite my best efforts. There are many other books that describe these atrocities in graphic detail. This book is not one of them.

This book will not discuss the political climate that was so ripe for the fall of Cambodia and the prevention of aid after the liberation at any length or the darker side of the genocide that turned Cambodians against each other, even among their own family. This book will tell some of my experiences and how I have healed and learned to find peace.

It is my sincere wish that reading this book will show that you, too, can find happiness and serenity regardless of your

circumstances. I hope you learn to seek and find good in every situation and live a life filled with joy, love, and abundance.
With all my love,
Pisey

Introduction

Even though forty years have passed since my family was torn apart and murdered by the Khmer Rouge, darkness still makes me so uncomfortable and nervous that I have to sleep with the light on. Even with my bedroom illuminated as brightly as a mid-summer day, I still hear the same sound in my nightmares. It's the sound of the struggle that started in the shallow pond by the makeshift hut my mom and I called home.

Mom and I knew exactly when the victim died as his groans, weakened with each blow from the folding chair, eventually ceased, and we heard his body splash into the pond. The road that prisoners were forced to walk on their way to their death ran directly in front of our hut, and we heard far too many such sounds. The victims were always taken away during the night.

The night was the scariest time as the darkness provided cover for the spies who were sent to report our activities to the Khmer Rouge's ruling body, Angkar. The only time I saw my mom was during the night; we were so terrified of the punishment inflicted on anybody who spoke against the Angkar and the villagers who were informants for the Khmer Rouge, we only spoke in hurried and guarded whispers even in our hut.

Before the fall of Cambodia on April 17, 1975, I lived in Phnom Penh with my mom, dad, and eleven-year-old brother, Rick. My father was a chemist who worked for an American pharmaceutical company, and my mom mostly stayed home with my brother and me. Our home was more than comfortable for our family and the many cousins who stayed with us when the Khmer Rouge conquered their village. Rick and I attended private school, and our home was happy and full of love.

On the night of April 16, 1975, my father learned that Phnom Penh was on the verge of occupation by the Khmer Rouge, and he was given the opportunity to escape by helicopter since he worked for an

American company. Dad chose to stay with us, and by the next morning, the Khmer Rouge had successfully conquered the city and begun the forced evacuation of two million people into the countryside.

Soldiers with loudspeakers announced that everybody had to leave the city for three days to allow the new government to settle and to pack enough supplies for the short trip. For the millions of Cambodians forced to evacuate the city, including the sick, the elderly, and children, it was the last time most of them saw Phnom Penh.

In four years, almost two million Cambodians died from execution, treachery and torture, starvation, exhaustion and the various, largely curable, diseases that ravaged the camps. All of Cambodia suffered during those four years, but those Cambodians forced from Phnom Penh endured an enormous loss of life.

Liberation is one of the most beautiful words man has ever created, and it will always send waves of gratitude rolling over me. Sadly, liberation also causes tremors of fear when I think back to the chaos, danger, and lawlessness that accompanied our liberation from the labor camps of the Khmer Rouge.

The second part of my journey began in 1979 when Cambodia was liberated by Vietnam. After four grueling years and the death of almost two million Cambodians, we were finally free. It was a miracle anyone survived the reign of terror, and we were determined to make the most of our gift of survival.

On January 7, 1979, I was working in the rice paddy field when we were ordered to evacuate. I was terrified when I realized the invading Vietnamese were so close, I could actually see their weapons. People were shouting for us to drop everything and run. I immediately stopped working and ran to the base to find my mother, who was working in a field approximately five kilometers away.

Everywhere I looked, people were running around trying to gather their family and meager belongings before they fled from the Vietnamese, whose invasion was primarily motivated by a desire to establish a pro-Vietnamese government. During the chaotic rush fleeing the labor camp, the only thoughts I had were of escape from the

Khmer Rouge and finding what remained of
my family.

I frantically searched for my mom and
was one of the last people to leave the base. I
was torn between the possibility of my death
if I waited and losing my mom if I left and
she stayed behind looking for me. It was far
too much for an eleven-year-old to think
clearly about.

Fear of dying alone on the abandoned base finally forced me to leave, and I
wasted no time escaping. I ran farther than
I thought my mom could have gone and
positioned myself to be certain to find her
since there was only one congested road
that led out of the camp and away from
the Vietnamese. I was successful, and we
were reunited and escaped from the Khmer
Rouge together.

Our harrowing escape was just the
beginning of our nine-year journey to freedom. We found my brother later the same
evening. Though we were technically free
from the Khmer Rouge, many of them
escaped from the Vietnamese, and we were
terrified not to obey their commands. We
no longer marched at gunpoint as we had
in Phnom Penh four years earlier, but the

Khmer Rouge still very much controlled our movements.

My journey from the official liberation of Cambodia to when I was actually free to live my life in my new country took nine years. I spent more than a year as an illegal refugee, and the refugee camps often did not provide much more security than the labor camps. Part two of this book shares some of my experiences during those nine years.

I do not share my story and its horrors to upset or shock you, although you may well feel these emotions. No child should ever have to endure such atrocities, and there can be no doubt that I lost my childhood innocence far too abruptly and prematurely.

I share my story with the hope that you find inspiration when you read Part Three of this book and become a wisdom seeker yourself. My experience growing up under the Khmer Rouge had the potential to destroy my mind and spirit like so many other survivors of the killing fields.

More than two decades since I began my new life in New Zealand, I feel nothing but gratitude for my life and experiences and love for all humanity. Forgiveness has healed my wounds and allowed me to experience true freedom, love, joy and abundance.

It might surprise you to learn that the lowest point in my life was not during the Khmer Rouge's four-year reign of terror or during my nine-year struggle to find a home where my family could live without fear. My lowest point was after my family settled in New Zealand.

I suddenly felt smothered by the freedom I fought so hard to achieve and alone in a world where I could not fit in anywhere. I was overwhelmed by the menial choices that most people take for granted. Every aspect of my life had been controlled for so long that I found myself unable to reach simple decisions. The freedom I fought so hard to achieve became a prison in my mind.

I soon found myself caught in a negative and destructive thought pattern that I could not escape. From the time I awoke, I would feel overwhelmed by the choices I had to make and would start the day berating myself for my inability to make a decision.

My negative thinking began to manifest in my physical body, and I began experiencing debilitating migraine headaches and stress-induced stomach problems. My life was going downhill quickly, and I just wanted to find some peace. I contemplated suicide to end the pain, but I knew I would dishonor the memory of my father and all those murdered in Cambodia if I took my life. I was lost.

That's when I began my search for meaning in my life. I discovered Napoleon Hill, Bob Proctor, Earl Nightingale and Robert Kiyosaki and many other great thinkers, and I began to search for goodness in every experience. As I looked for the good in life, it became obvious to me that it had been there all along just waiting to be discovered.

The serenity I now enjoy did not happen overnight. I spent many years running from the memories of my childhood. It was not until I allowed myself to seek happiness that I was able to fully experience the joy and abundance I now enjoy.

Part three of this book will help you understand yourself more and to find the goodness in your own life's experience. When you master the 4P method I share in this part, you will become a wisdom seeker yourself and enjoy all the benefits of a peaceful, serene, and truly wealthy life.

Part One

"I shall never forget how I was roused one night by the groans of a fellow prisoner, who threw himself about in his sleep, obviously having a horrible nightmare. Since I had always been especially sorry for people who suffered from fearful dreams or deliria, I ʷᵃⁿᵗᵉᵈ ᵗᵒ ʷᵃᵏᵉ ᵗʰᵉ ᵖᵒᵒʳ ᵐᵃⁿ. *Suddenly I drew back the hand which was ready to shake him, frightened at the thing I was about to do. At that moment I became intensely conscious of the fact that no dream, no matter how horrible, could be as bad as the reality of the camp which surrounded us, and to which I was about to recall him."* ~Viktor E. Frankl, *Man's Search for Meaning*

Chapter 1
Marked for Death

The increasingly loud sounds from artillery fire during the conspicuously absent three-day Cambodian New Year's celebration in 1975 told everybody that Phnom Penh was going to be taken within a few days. On April 16, 1975, Dad moved my mom, my brother Rick and me to the center of the city to our uncle's house, so we would be with our extended family as a larger group when the Khmer Rouge captured our city.

Though I have never been sure why my dad's position with the Americans made him leave us at my uncle's house and return to work that afternoon, there must have been a very good reason he left, and I knew better than to question him. I was frightened by the move to my uncle's house and the obvious concern on my father's face, but I was more frightened as the hours ticked by and Dad did not return. As the night dragged on, we anxiously waited for him and any information his job with the Americans provided.

The morning of April 17 was eerily quiet and tense on the streets of Phnom Penh, and Dad still had not returned. The government imposed a curfew, and our fear kept us inside all night until the Khmer Rouge's tanks began slowly rolling through the city. Nervous tension and uncertainty were evident on the faces of everyone around me, and I was so relieved and surprised when the celebrating began.

"Look, Mom," I said with delight as I saw the first soldier with a beautiful flower in the muzzle of his rifle. "They aren't going to hurt us!" The tension on Mom's face was quickly replaced by confusion as a tank carrying one of our beloved Buddhist monks waving at the people now cheering from their windows rolled by. The convoy of military vehicles resembled a St. Patrick's Day parade as people began to cheer and wave to the soldiers like they would wave to the people riding on the floats in a parade.

All around me, people were emerging from their homes and celebrating. The fighting was over, and the Khmer Rouge had come in peace! Soldiers waved at the crowds, and people began tossing flowers and shouting praise for the Khmer Rouge from their second and third story windows.

For the first time in days, our friends and neighbors celebrated in the streets, and we stood on the balcony waving at the troops because we were finally free from the dark cloud of fear that governed every part of our lives. It was such a confusing event for me because I knew that my dad moved us from our home into our uncle's home because he feared the Khmer Rouge, yet the atmosphere surrounding me was that of liberated people celebrating.

My celebration was short lived and my confusion justified when I spotted my dad weaving through the tanks and crowds of people on his brand new Vespa scooter. Even from a distance, I could tell by his expression of panic that something was very wrong.

As he got closer, he began shouting to us, "Find something white to show surrender! Wave something white!" I remember my mom scrambling and saying we didn't have a white flag. I did not understand the urgency until we heard the voices of the Khmer Rouge soldiers booming through their megaphones moments later. They sounded very tense and angry, and I recall hearing them shout something like, "Phnom Penh has fallen! Surrender your weapons and display a white flag to show surrender, or you will be considered hostile to the revolution!"

My fear grew as I saw the piles of AK-47 rifles accumulating from the government soldiers who joined the procession of Khmer Rouge tanks and soldiers. My fear turned into terror as I heard gunshots and explosions followed by screaming and shouting.

The party-like atmosphere quickly turned into one of chaos. People were running and screaming as the Khmer Rouge began herding the people whose homes were on the ground level into the road and marching them away at gunpoint. Those who showed resistance or did not move fast enough were shot immediately.

Even at the age of seven, I knew we were in grave danger. My dad made it into my uncle's apartment and ordered us away from the windows. We did not leave Phnom Penh like most people on April 17. Instead, we passed the day and night hiding in silence and fear as the adults considered our options. They must have known we would have to leave, but the sights and sounds of death were so frightening that leaving was the last thing they wanted for us.

Nonetheless, in the early hours of April 18, we left our refuge loaded with our belongings on my dad's new scooter and the supplies we thought we needed for the three-day period and joined the millions of Cambodians marching. I suppose my father knew it was unlikely that the Khmer Rouge would allow us to return after three days, but he did not reveal his knowledge to my brother and me, and we left our uncle's home thinking we would return.

The evacuation we were told would last for the three days the Khmer Rouge needed to reorganize the former government into the so-called democratic government of Kampuchea turned into a death march that lasted for more than three months. At first, we covered almost no ground and were essentially stuck in one place for hours as the road was too congested to allow movement. The first few nights we spent on the road, there was not even enough room to lie down and stretch out our bodies.

When I consider the distance we traveled between the city and our first labor camp in Angchot, I am struck by the senselessness of the march. The entire trip would take ninety minutes by car, yet we were ordered to take certain routes that made the trip drag on for months.

As the days turned into weeks, the sick and many of the elderly died as we marched toward the countryside. Food and water were scarce, and the heat led to the demise of many. Our money was almost worthless, and the jewelry my very resourceful mother had packed quickly dwindled as she traded our gold for necessities with local villagers. We were told to leave the bodies on the side of the road for the Khmer Rouge to bury. The sight of the dead and dying became so common that I would hardly notice them anymore because I was trying so hard to keep up and stay with my family.

Somewhere during the first few days of walking on the road, I heard that the Khmer Rouge would separate our family farther along. We were told that my dad would have to go to work at one camp, my mother would be taken to another camp, and my brother and I would be assigned to separate labor camps.

The thought of being separated from my parents was scary, but the thought of Dad being taken from us was terrifying. My dad and I were especially close, and I was always what you would call a Daddy's Girl. My dad never expected me to be the traditionally submissive Cambodian girl and encouraged me to follow my heart and believe in myself. I knew there was no way I could survive without my father.

One of my most vivid memories of the march away from Phnom Penh was a night when my dad shook me awake from a nightmare. I dreamed that the Khmer Rouge took my beloved dad away, and I had been crying in my sleep. I remember begging my father to ask the soldiers not to separate us. I cried, "Please, Dad, ask them to keep us together. Tell the soldiers that I cannot live without you!"

How my dad's heart must have broken as I wept and begged. My father knew he had no control over what would happen to our family and that he and my brother would likely be separated from Mom and me. We had already been forcefully driven from our home, made to sleep on roads, and endure the sweltering heat of our Cambodian summer. If Dad had any hope about favorable conditions for his family before the capture of Phnom Penh, after the first three days on the road he must have known that we were completely at the mercy of the Khmer Rouge. Our lives were in their hands and the hands of the many millions of Cambodians the Khmer Rouge empowered.

For the first time in my life, I saw my father openly weep as he held me and tried unsuccessfully to comfort me. As he held me, my sobbing woke my mother and brother and we passed the night holding and consoling each other. We wept for the loss we had already endured and the wonderful life we'd been forced to leave behind. We wept for the misery and torment the Khmer Rouge made us endure on the journey from Phnom Penh. Mostly, we wept for the future that we knew would be stolen from us. Our life was being torn apart, and we were powerless to put it back together.

"What a cruel thing war is ... to fill our hearts with hatred instead of love for our neighbors." ~Robert E. Lee

Chapter 2
The Best and the Worst of the Occupation

When I look back at my life growing up under the Khmer Rouge, I realize that my eighth birthday passed sometime during the months we spent on the death march from Phnom Penh. We were grateful for our very survival as a family during those months, and when we finally arrived in the village of Angchot, celebration of any kind was not an option.

We were much more fortunate than many who were forced from their homes in the city because my mom was raised in the village of Angchot, and my uncle's family still lived there and allowed us to move into his home. When we arrived at my uncle's house, I was shocked and dismayed by their home, which did not have electricity, running water, or toilet facilities.

For a brief time, I felt very sorry for my uncle and his family for being so poor. My sympathy quickly turned into anger when my four-year-old cousin scornfully told me about his shame and resentment for the association with my family. In retrospect, that shame and resentment was somewhat justified since the mere association with my family resulted in the torture and subsequent deaths of several other cousins who would likely have reached very high ranks in the Khmer Rouge were they not burdened with relatives from the city.

As confusing and painful as my cousin's resentment was, within days I understood that my family belonged to a group of people who had become the lowest form of life in all of Cambodia; our lives were no longer valuable to anyone other than ourselves. As long as we were profitable to the new regime, we were permitted to live. Our worth as human beings was measured in grains of rice.

Villages that were occupied by the Khmer Rouge before the official establishment of Pol Pot's communist government suffered varying degrees of turmoil. All villagers were forced to surrender their livestock and eventually their crops to the Khmer Rouge, but they were permitted to remain in their homes. My family and all others driven from the city were called newcomers and forced to leave our relatives' homes and move into tiny huts that housed two families separated only by a thin wall. Though they helped us by sneaking us food when they could, any association with a newcomer was damning, and some members of my mother's family were not saddened by our forced relocation to the flimsy and crowded huts that were erected for us.

From four in the morning until late into the evening, my family worked in the fields farming rice. Despite the excruciatingly long hours of labor in the fields, which included meager rations of wheat that we were hardly able to stomach and constant fear of death, this was the best period I can recall from my life under the Khmer Rouge. My family was alive, and we were together.

This six-month period marked the beginning of the psychological torture new-comers endured. Each month, we would have to attend gatherings where we would sit in rows on the ground and mechanically raise our fist and shout, "Angkar!" in a perverse gesture of support for the Khmer Rouge. Even though we knew the Angkar were responsible for our suffering, we knew better than to respond to the brainwashing with anything less than feigned enthusiasm since experience quickly taught us that an unenthusiastic response would lead to torture or even death. There were always people taken to their deaths after these meetings. I am not ashamed to admit we were far too afraid of being the next to be executed to protest the murder of people we suspected of being no more guilty of crimes against Angkar than us.

During these monthly meetings, we would listen to Khmer Rouge leaders talk of the equality that the revolution would bring to Cambodia. The leaders would explain how moving the rich city dwellers into the country would bring more balance between the peasants and the affluent and make everyone equal. The leaders would tell us the Angkar planned to harvest three tons of rice per hectare of land by building irrigation channels and harvesting three times a year, even though these estimations were absurd to almost everyone present.

Despite the absurdity of their claims and the open hostility the Khmer Rouge felt toward us, we showed as much enthusiasm as we could muster toward the Angkar and the prosperity they hoped to achieve at our expense. The Khmer Rouge blamed the newcomers for Cambodia's turmoil and not so subtly encouraged local villagers to abuse and torment us in the name of Angkar.

In addition to the monthly brainwashing gatherings, there were smaller weekly meetings led by the villagers appointed by the Khmer Rouge where we would openly criticize each other. Each newcomer would be forced to accuse someone else of some transgression against Angkar, and the accused would have to accept the criticism and promise to atone and correct the transgression. When there were no transgressions to report, we made them up for fear of being accused of disloyalty to Angkar for not criticizing our neighbors.

The last recording made by ousted Prince Sihanouk when he was in China was played at one of the monthly meetings where he encouraged us, his "children of Cambodia," to remain strong and join the Khmer Rouge. It saddens me when I remember how many of the newcomers were excited to hear the voice of their prince, only to realize that the Khmer Rouge had deceived him as well as many others. The recording I remember so vividly was made shortly before the Khmer Rouge murdered most of the prince's family.

I realize now that the Khmer Rouge massacre was fueled by deception and fear. The Khmer Rouge gave disgruntled and poor people hope for a utopian society at the expense of the perceived affluent. Many Cambodians were victimized and brainwashed into believing that nobody could be trusted, and it became a self-fulfilling prophecy. People who might have supported one another and been allies against the genocide instead became enemies and reported minor so-called transgressions against the Party to the Angkar, which directly resulted in the offender being severely punished or killed.

Sadly, many newcomers were tortured and lost their lives to settle personal vendettas in the name of the Khmer Rouge. This disturbing fact may surprise you, as it seems to be largely overlooked in the annals of history. Nonetheless, I cannot possibly share my message and honor the victims of the genocide without acknowledging many of the senseless deaths that were the result of false accusations. It is obvious to the world that the Khmer Rouge victimized all of Cambodia, but in the six months I spent in Angchot, I quickly learned to fear my fellow Cambodians as much as I feared Angkar.

"The greatest threat to peace is the barrage of rightist propaganda portraying war as decent, honorable, and patriotic."
~Jeanette Rankin

Chapter 3
Angkar Needs You

Pol Pot and the leaders of the Khmer Rouge were masters of deception and false diplomacy. Through the use of deception, they convinced almost seven hundred thousand Cambodian peasants to turn against their fellow countrymen and join the Khmer Rouge revolution. As a well-educated and well-versed leader, Pol Pot even managed to convince ousted Prince Sihanouk of an alliance between the communist Khmer Rouge and the monarch.

Our village leader was also a very skilled orator, and his gently persuading voice induced as much fear as did the harsh shouting from the largely teenage and viciously unforgiving Khmer Rouge guards. The leader was always calm and seemingly sincere when he would tell the newcomers that the

Angkar needed them for the various, largely white-collar, positions they occupied in the past. We dreaded to hear that Angkar needed anybody because those who answered the call usually vanished during the night.

The young Khmer Rouge soldiers were merciless when punishing any so-called crime against the Angkar. It was not uncommon to see someone tied to a tree and left in the sweltering sun for days before they were released, perished, or executed. Aside from punishment for a crime against the Angkar where public punishment was used to deter others from repeating the offense or considering a transgression of their own, the Angkar was always portrayed as gentle and welcoming. They tried to hide most of their crimes under the cover of darkness.

I was always amazed by the village leader's ability to lie so effortlessly during the monthly propaganda meetings. The newcomers in the audience were the very people who suffered the most under the Khmer Rouge, yet our leader would speak about our collective achievements and pleasing the Angkar with complete sincerity. Despite their unparalleled brutality and blatant disregard for human life, we were always told that

Angkar was our family. We did not need any of the old ways because the Angkar would provide us with everything we needed.

My family was lucky in comparison to many other families because we got to spend six months after the fall of Cambodia together. Many families from the city who were forced to relocate to other villages lost their fathers to what the Khmer Rouge called re-education almost immediately upon arrival. Re-education was the Khmer Rouge's term for torture followed by execution. I learned from the other children in a work group long after my dad had been executed that their fathers had been taken away only days after the death march from Phnom Penh.

My family's separation began during one of our monthly meetings in Angchot where we heard our village leader say the dreaded words, "Angkar needs strong men to volunteer." Angkar needed the men for a mobile group to build irrigation canals. The words sent shivers down my spine as I listened because I knew it meant Dad was being sent away. In a gentle, kind, and convincing voice, the leader explained that the men would be too far away to return home at night, but food and water would be plentiful, and the men would be allowed to return for visits. The description sounded almost like a holiday compared to the life we lived in huts just outside of Angchot.

No one dared question the leader since we noticed many people vanish into the night for lesser offenses than ignoring the Angkar's call. I knew my dad's time had come, and our family would be separated. We did not believe that life would be any better for my dad after he joined the work group, but Dad knew he would be killed if he did not volunteer. Dad also knew his chances of survival were slim considering his status as a newcomer and the number of men being killed by the Khmer Rouge. Dad answered the Angkar's call and set out to increase his slim chance of survival by working hard and showing his value.

My dad's departure for his work group was excruciatingly painful. Any display of emotion was prohibited since it showed a family connection and, therefore, a lack of loyalty to our new family: the Angkar. I knew I might not see my dad again, and hiding my feelings was almost impossible.

After Dad left, it seemed much less likely to me that we would survive.

Our days were painfully long and filled with misery. Not long after Dad left Angchot, my brother was sent to the boys' mobile group away from us in the opposite direction. The pain of losing my brother so quickly after my father had to join a similar group nearly incapacitated my mother and me. We longed for our family to be back together and feared for their safety.

To our amazement, the Angkar remained true to their word and allowed our family to be reunited for one, bittersweet evening of celebration. When I first saw my father, I was so filled with joy that I did not notice how thin he'd become. I saw that he was wearing the crudely made sandals that the teenage guards wore and knew he'd gained the favor of one of the guards. I was filled with hope for the future.

When we were finally alone and out of hearing range of the guards, my mom asked my dad how things were for him at his new camp. The conditions he described were nothing like those he was promised. Like us, his day began long before sunrise and did not end until well into the night. The promised abundance of food and water had not materialized, and they barely survived on the twice a day ration of a watery bowl of rice. My dad had already suffered from several bouts of debilitating stomach ailments and was frightfully thin.

Despite the adversity he faced in his new labor camp, my dad was grateful to be alive, and we were all thankful for the brief reunion. The reunion gave us an opportunity to be together and bask from the warmth of our love for each other. Sadly, the reunion also confirmed what we already knew: there was little hope of our lives improving as long as the Khmer Rouge was in command of Cambodia.

My dad and brother were sent back to their respective camps the next morning, and Mom and I were filled with unspoken dread as we each wondered if we would see them again. Our quality of life was getting worse by the day, and we were powerless to do anything to make improvements.

Less than two months after our bittersweet reunion, my mom received news that my dad had been taken away and killed. The sandals fashioned from automobile tires that gave me a fleeting glimmer of hope were my dad's way of telling Mom he was going to be murdered. While working in the kitchen that now fed only the elite Khmer Rouge, my mom received his sandals as his final goodbye.

"No one saves us but ourselves. No one can and no one may. We ourselves must walk the path." ~Buddha

Chapter 4
Keep Moving and Look Away

It is difficult to remember and think about all the death and suffering that surrounded me during the four years of Pol Pot's command. I remember how shocked and horrified I was the first time I saw human remains. It was the body of an elderly woman on the side of the road during the march from Phnom Penh, and my dad had to drag me physically as he tried to console me and keep my obvious shock hidden from the Khmer Rouge guards who were everywhere.

I pointed, started to cry, and stopped walking partially because I was so shocked by the sight of a dead person and also because I could not believe we were just going to leave the lady's body there like she was garbage. As my whispers to my father began to turn into hysterical sobs, he started to drag me while whispering, "Just keep moving, Pisey. Look away and everything will be okay! Keep moving, Pisey. Look away and everything will be okay."

Those few words from my father became a life-saving motto that I chanted countless times to myself over the next four years. Whenever I saw somebody being punished or taken away, I would silently repeat my dad's words and tell myself to keep moving, look away, and everything would be okay. Life was far from okay, and survival was the best we could hope for. Nonetheless, those words from my father reminded me to stay silent if I wanted to stay alive. Those words from my father saved me many times.

Even though I was only seven years old, I quickly learned to control my reaction to the pain and death that became unwanted companions in my life. Within a few short months after leaving Phnom Penh, it was evident that death was the norm and life was an exception.

The Khmer Rouge motto, "To spare you is no profit, to destroy you is no loss" did not adequately reflect the danger we faced.

As newcomers from the city, destroying us was a pleasure for many who were brainwashed into believing we were the sole cause of every problem the country faced from poverty and famine to corruption and war. We were constantly scrutinized by villagers who hoped to gain the favor of the Khmer Rouge by reporting us for crimes against the Angkar. Many newcomers lost their lives for petty offenses made from an honest lack of knowledge, and many more lost their lives for simply being present when the guards were looking for someone to kill.

After my dad and brother had been taken away, mom and I lived in a tiny hut where we held each other every night trying to exchange enough strength to survive another day. Our hut was close to the main walking path where the Khmer Rouge marched the people being taken for torture and execution. We heard the muffled protests of prisoners being shoved toward their cruel fate almost every night, and my dad's words coupled with my mom's soothing arms kept me silent many times.

The night that still haunts my dreams was a particularly horrific night as a fight broke out just in front of our hut. Mom and I were asleep when we heard the distinct sound of people getting kicked and punched. Mom held me tight, and I started chanting in my head, "Keep moving and look away. Keep moving and look away." Obviously, there was nothing for me to see, but it was the reminder I needed to stay silent.

The scuffle moved from the path to the shallow pond mere feet from the entrance to our hut. We heard splashing, grunting, and groaning as the fight continued. I felt my mom's arms tighten around me as her breathing became shallow. We were so frightened.

As the fighting continued, we heard the footsteps of more people running toward our hut and into the pond. Then we heard the first thud of a metal object connecting with a human body. All other sounds ceased except for the victim's cry of pain. THUD! We heard the sound again followed by a muffled cry from the victim. THUD, THUD, THUD, THUD followed by silence, and a splash as the victim collapsed into the water.

By this time, my lungs were screaming for air from holding my breath, but I was too terrified of being noticed by the people yielding the metal object of death to breathe. When I could no longer hold my breath, I inhaled the tiniest amount of air I could without making a sound and began a kind of silent, rhythmic chanting ritual in my head to keep myself from screaming. "Little breath, keep moving. Little breath, look away. Little breath, keep moving. Little breath, look away."

As we shook in terror, we heard the distinct sound of the victim being dragged from the water and onto the path as his murderers grumbled and cursed him. My heart pounded as we listened to the sound of the body being dragged away, and the night grew silent. I continued my silent chanting and breathing routine until I felt my mother's vise-like grip on me loosen slightly, and she slowly exhaled.

I tried to speak, but my mom's expression kept me silent. I think Mom knew how close I was to complete hysteria, and she refused to draw any unwanted attention to our hut. Experience taught us that unwilling witnesses to the Khmer Rouge's crimes were often silenced by their disappearance into the night.

As my mom held me and silently stroked my hair, exhaustion finally got the best of me, and I drifted off into a fitful and restless sleep. I dreamed of the faceless victim and his demise that night and for many nights after. The sounds of the fight outside our hut echoed in my head and dominated my dreams.

The following morning, the only evidence of the crime we heard the night before was the scuffmarks in the dirt. It was obvious that there was an unusual amount of movement around the entrance to our hut and that someone or something had been dragged away.

Later that day, one of the cooks in the kitchen told my mom that one of the newcomers who had been highly skilled in martial arts had disappeared the night before. Mom and I concluded that he chose not to go quietly or without a fight and silently applauded his efforts and prayed for his spirit's safe journey home.

About three weeks after the incident, I had all but forgotten about the brave man and his last stand when there was a particularly heavy rainfall. As I trotted toward the small pond by our hut, I noticed something sticking out of the ground. I cautiously approached the unusual object and found myself caught somewhere between shock and terror as I realized it was the body of the victim who had been unearthed from his shallow grave by the heavy rainfall.

My mouth flew open to scream, but my dad's words started running through my head, "Keep moving, Pisey. Look away and everything will be okay. Keep moving, Pisey. Look away and everything will be okay." I somehow controlled my screams and ran back into the hut. Dad's words saved me again.

The fight outside our hut is just one of the reasons I suffer from occasional nightmares and insomnia. I sleep with the bedroom lights on, and when the sounds intrude on my dreams, my heartbeat still races for what seems like a very long time after. I think of that man and the other millions of victims on those nights as sleep eludes me. I thank God for sparing my family and pray for the peaceful rest of those who were not as fortunate.

"Tricks and treachery are the practice of fools who don't have brains enough to be honest." ~Benjamin Franklin

Chapter 5
Stolen Salt

Of the two million people forced to leave Phnom Penh, less than five hundred thousand survived. Mom's resourcefulness, determination, and strength saved our lives. There were many times when she gave me food from the kitchen when I would sneak into her camp to visit; she never faltered in her eagerness to prove her worth to the Khmer Rouge, and when there was a job nobody wanted to do, my mom was the first to volunteer.

Not long after we arrived in the village of Anghot, Mom was forced to join an all-women's labor camp whose job was to collect human waste and turn it into fertilizer. Not surprisingly, this was considered the lowest and most undesirable task and was assigned to the newcomers.

As instructed by the Angkar, each home in the village constructed a toilet, which consisted of a platform with a hole leading to a clay urn that collected the urine and feces. The women in my mom's group had to collect the urns and bring it to the base camp to make fertilizer.

The experiment was disgusting and difficult, but Mom was determined to enhance her chances of survival by increasing her worth to the Khmer Rouge. My mom did the work and was quickly recognized for her work ethic, despite being a newcomer.

Mom was given a small plot of land and two bulls with which she was to grow vegetables using the experimental fertilizer. The work was difficult, and failure to produce a crop would have likely resulted in execution, but Mom persevered and successfully produced an abundance of vegetables despite the difficulties she faced such as having to carry water for the crops over long distances.

One of the Khmer Rouge leaders noticed Mom's effort and strong work ethic, and she was rewarded by being appointed the duty of producing vegetables for the kitchen that now fed only the privileged villagers and high-ranking Khmer Rouge officials passing through since the newcomers had all been sent to labor camps.

After a disgruntled cousin, who lost his opportunity for advancement in the Khmer Rouge because of his association with our family, complained to the authority about Mom's slightly elevated status, my mother was removed from the position and sent to join the other newcomers.

Mom worked in the labor camps for almost a year until her former superior was promoted and requested that Mom be relocated to her area on the basis that her ability to produce vegetables was unmatched. The Angkar granted the request, and Mom spent the remainder of the occupation growing vegetables in Angchot.

The leader knew that Mom was honest and hardworking, and they developed a strong bond based on mutual respect and love for family. The leader had three small children, and her husband was away for months without visiting. Mom often helped her care for her children, and the leader overlooked my presence when I was supposed to be working at my children's labor camp but ran away to see my mom instead.

Despite the honest hard work and monumental effort my mom made, treachery was a very real part of the genocide, and my mother almost lost her life because of this dark and largely unspoken part of the Khmer Rouge's occupation.

My mother was resourceful in and out of the kitchen. When there was something that an elite member of the Angkar requested that required special ingredients that were unavailable, Mom was the person the cooks asked for help. It was not unusual for my mom to be roused from her sleep to secretly aid the chef in preparing a special meal for the Angkar.

My mom worked closely with a husband and wife team who were the official vegetable grower and fisherman for the kitchen. The couple was Khmer Rouge but became dear friends of my mom's and jokingly called her their in-law.

In preparation for a very high-ranking member of the Angkar, Mom was requested to make the Cambodian delicacy: savory pancakes. The woman with whom Mom worked side-by-side every day was pregnant and asked Mom to bring her some of the pancakes.

My mom's position was delicate, and her participation in food preparation had to be kept secret since she was a newcomer. Mom reminded her friend that bringing her a treat would result in her execution and as Khmer Rouge, she and her husband could enjoy the delicacy without her involvement.

Several weeks later, the fisherman asked Mom if she would go to the tightly controlled storage shed and request a bowl of salt with which he planned to preserve some fish. Mom obliged without question and was given the requested salt, which she brought to our hut to keep for the fisherman.

My mom had not seen her friends for several days when she returned to our hut to discover the salt had been stolen. I remember the sadness in my mom's eyes as she understood the betrayal by the fisherman and his wife, and she quietly told me, "I refused to bring her the pancakes, and now I have been framed."

My mom was in serious trouble, and if it were not for her honest and trustworthy leader along with the collaborating lies of the head of the kitchen, the vengeful plot against my mother would have been successful. Not only had the fisherman stolen the salt from our hut, he reported to the Angkar that my mom had stolen it for her personal use.

My mom explained her situation to her leader, who knew Mom would not steal anything, and the leader launched an investigation into the accusation. After a very tense few days, the head of the kitchen arrived at our hut carrying a bowl of salt that he claimed was to replace the salt he had borrowed from the hut.

The chef claimed he'd run out of salt and needed to prepare food, so he had taken Mom's supply without asking since she was working in the fields. The chef apologized profusely for the confusion, and saved my mom's life with his lie.

The fisherman and his wife were never accused of any deception; as such an accusation would have incriminated the chef and my mom's leader. Indeed, the couple worked with my mom for the remainder of the occupation, and through my mother's amazing poise of character, the incident was never mentioned.

It is human nature to want more, to want to be more than your neighbors, and to lash out at those who fail to do as you wish. Human nature often has a very ugly side that creates catastrophic situations when the opportunity arises like Pol Pot and his Khmer Rouge.

I share this story not just to demonstrate the dark side of human nature or the blatant disregard for our lives but also to show that there were some very decent and honest people who were Khmer Rouge. However misguided they may have been, many of the Khmer Rouge genuinely believed they were helping Cambodia during the occupation. There were honest and kind Khmer Rouge like the chef and Mom's leader, who risked their lives to save Mom's.

"A hungry man can't see right or wrong. He just sees food." ~Pearl S. Buck

Chapter 6
Starving for Mom

My youth was both a blessing and a curse during the Khmer Rouge's occupation. I was young and not punished as severely as I would have been if I were an older child or an adult when I ran away from my labor group to see my mom. Though my attachment to my mom was frowned upon and officially seen as disloyal to the Angkar, it was tolerated, and I seldom received any discipline for the many times I escaped my work group and ran back to my mother's hut. I was fortunate that Mom had earned her position and had a close bond with her leader. If other Khmer Rouge leaders had discovered me, the outcome of my visits to my mom would likely have been severe punishment or death.

The downside of being young was my decreased value to the Khmer Rouge. A starving nine-year-old from the city was not particularly useful in the world of manual labor and farming. Like my mom, when we first arrived in Angchot, I tried my best to increase my chances of survival by working hard and doing the work that nobody else wanted to do. Still, I was young, frightened and inexperienced, and there were many occasions when the others in my group had to help me finish my work so we could return to our huts for the night.

It was almost a year before I was sent away from my mother to join an all-girls' labor camp. Before that, I looked after myself during the day, and Mom would care for me in the evenings and cuddle and soothe me at night. But from the time I was nine, I worked from four in the morning until well into the night in the fields. I missed my mom so much that it was unbearable to face each day without her comforting ways and encouragement.

The work my group did was tedious, and though it was not considered hard labor in comparison to what the adults did during their workday, it was difficult for a nine-year-old and the extended work hours fueled by two rations of watery rice left me near collapse.

Like most newcomers who had not been executed or died from hunger, exhaustion, or one of the often-curable diseases that ravaged the camps, I was slowly starving to death. Edema caused my limbs to swell to where I thought my skin would break.

The constant hunger and preoccupation with finding something to satisfy the incessant gnawing in my stomach was all consuming. I lived in a hut with ten other girls who belonged to the same group. At four in the morning, the guards would wake us, and we would begin work in the field either planting or harvesting rice or gathering animal dung to make fertilizer.

It was always six to eight hours before we received our first daily ration, and by that time, I would be ravenous. I spent my days looking for anything I could find to eat. I ate snails, frogs, shrimp, leaves, lizards and anything else that looked like it might keep the hunger away for a few minutes. I was so hungry and preoccupied with finding something that would satisfy my craving that finding a small lizard or snail was a cause for celebration. I remember the few times I was lucky enough to catch a lizard, thinking about eating it later made the entire day more bearable.

Thoughts of food and hunger clouded my thoughts and often impaired my judgment. On one occasion, I found some leaves that I decided to cook and eat. They must have given me food poisoning because I awoke the following morning covered in my vomit. The stench lasted for weeks since there were no facilities to properly clean my things or myself. It probably would have taught me a lesson if I were not starving because I went back to foraging for what I hoped would be edible leaves soon after.

Every night as I lay on my filthy mat, I would picture my mom and long for the comfort of her arms around me. When the pain of her absence got to be too much, I would sneak away during the night and run to her hut. Mom was always so happy to see me but so saddened by my appearance. On one visit, Mom was shocked by how much I had deteriorated. My hair was full of lice, my teeth were all blackened, and I was frighteningly thin. My mom shaved my head and did her best to clean me up. Mom always had a small piece of fruit or a vegetable for me to eat when I visited, and I must admit, knowing I would get a reprieve from the constant pain in my stomach motivated many stolen visits with my mom. I was starved for her love and attention, and I was starved for the small amounts of life-sustaining food she would give me.

The constant hunger that occupied my every thought and was never satisfied became the very reason I left my group for good. Mornings were always the hardest for me because we were roused from our sleep at four, and the painful gnawing would begin. My first thought every morning would be, "What can I find to eat? I must find something to eat." These thoughts would bounce around repeatedly for hours and hours until we were given out first ration of watery rice porridge.

As soon as the hunger was temporarily satisfied and the nagging voices in my head stopped telling me to find something to eat, I began thinking about Mom and how much I missed her and wished we could be together. It would not be long before the hunger pains returned and hijacked my thoughts. One evening, I somehow found

the self-discipline to save some of my ration
for the morning. Though it felt as though I
would not be able to sleep from the hunger
and the knowledge that food was available,
I forced myself to sleep knowing that food
in the morning was going to be sweeter than
any food I could ever enjoy at night.

I drifted off to sleep imagining the
feeling of heading to the fields with food in
my stomach and was full of pride that I had
mastered my hunger and myself. When I
woke up the following morning and looked
eagerly for my rice, all I found was an empty
bowl. One of the girls with whom I shared
the hut had stolen and eaten my rice. I was
devastated!

Logic told me whoever had eaten the
rice could not have helped herself because
she was starving, too, but it was one of the
lowest points for me. I was so proud of my
plan, so disappointed by the betrayal, and
now faced another morning of labor hun-
grier than I'd ever been because I did not eat
the last ration. I decided then I was going
to go and stay with my mom, or I would
die trying. I'd had enough of the starvation,
hard labor, abuse and now this betrayal.

I escaped from my work group and took my usual route to find my mom. As usual, she was torn between joy when she saw me and terror for the possible repercussions of my running away. She greeted me with a huge hug, all the while telling me I should not have come. It was heaven, and I knew that home was wherever Mom was.

Thanks to Mom's close relationship with her leader, I was unofficially allowed to stay, or at least, not sent back to my labor group. Within a few months, I belonged to the group of children working in the village and got to spend my nights in the hut with my mom.

It was a far cry from the life we'd known before the Khmer Rouge occupation, but for me, it was paradise. Food was far from plentiful, but I was much more comfortable than I had been for many years. I was no longer starving for food or my mom, and that was more than enough reason to be grateful.

Part Two

"A good plan violently executed is better than a perfect plan executed next week."
~George S. Patton

Chapter 7
Our Liberation

There are many academic reports that refer to the Vietnamese intervention to overthrow Pol Pot and the Khmer Rouge as an invasion rather than liberation. Without question, the Vietnamese invasion of Cambodia was politically motivated, and they remained in Cambodia for ten years after the liberation. The Vietnamese invasion was a direct response to multiple attacks by the Khmer Rouge against Vietnam. These are undisputed facts.

Hundreds of thousands of Cambodians continued to die from starvation and largely curable diseases long after the liberation. Vietnam signed a treaty of friendship with the former Soviet Union in 1978. While the friendship treaty offered the Vietnamese some assurance of protection from China for the invasion of Cambodia, it also created a conflict of interest for the Western world and the United Nations, whose aid was desperately needed and largely absent. These are undisputed facts.

Hundreds of thousands more Cambodians died attempting to flee the country and escape the fighting that continued in many parts of Cambodia. For many of the Khmer Rouge soldiers and their families that escaped into the jungle, their protective jungle became their deathbed as they were trapped without food or supplies of any kind for more than three months before the Vietnamese permitted them to seek asylum in neighboring Thailand. These are undisputed facts.

Regardless of the political motivation or lack thereof by the rest of the world in aiding the millions of Cambodians in desperate need, my heart is full of gratitude when I think back to the day of our liberation from the Khmer Rouge. I would not have survived for much longer under the Khmer Rouge. Like most of the surviving newcomers, I was starving, sick, and on the brink of death. This is an undisputable fact.

The official day of liberation is cited as January 7, 1979. I have no way of knowing if this is accurate since we measured the passage of time in seasons, death, and labor camps: two seasons since Dad died or three seasons in the girls' labor group. Regardless of the date, it is a day I will always remember as one of the most joyful and confusing in my entire life.

The day began like most others at four in the morning. I was working in my all-girls' labor group in the rice field when people began shouting for us to drop everything and run from the invading Vietnamese. I looked up from my work and was terrified to see soldiers with weapons pointed in my direction advancing toward the field where we worked.

As I ran toward our hut, hoping to find my mom, I was terrified by the chaos that surrounded me. People were running everywhere trying to find their families and gather their belongings. Newcomers, privileged villagers, and Khmer Rouge alike were all scurrying about trying to get supplies and escape the Vietnamese invaders. The rumors we heard prior to the Vietnamese action against the Khmer Rouge told us the

Vietnamese soldiers would not spare the life of any Cambodian whether they were Khmer Rouge or civilians.

I was not surprised when I could not find my mom since she was working about five kilometers from the base and would not have made it back yet. People were shouting at me to run with them as they hurried away, but I did not want to leave without my mom.

I was scared and confused. I wanted to run with the others to escape the fighting, but I was afraid my mother would return from the vegetable field, wait for me, and get caught in the fighting herself. It was, without question, one of the worst times I can remember and the most helpless I felt.

Fear of dying alone on the abandoned base made me leave, and it was easy for me to get ahead of the crowd. We all traveled on the same road since it was the only road leading away from the fighting. Even though the road was very congested, I had no belongings to carry, I was alone, and I was much smaller than most people, so it was easy for me to weave around groups of people trying to stay together. My absolute determination to find Mom in the crowd also helped propel me through the masses until I was a safe distance from the base.

I positioned myself where I would be sure to see her as she approached and began scanning the crowd. After what seemed like a lifetime, I was elated to see her familiar figure carrying one small pot toward the end of the line. It was a joyful reunion. We embraced and cried with joy despite the chaos that surrounded us and began the next part of our journey toward freedom together.

Our first destination was the village where we thought we would find my brother. That village had not been ordered to evacuate, but the leader was an honest and dignified man who allowed my brother to join us. We spent the first night in almost four years together at a cousin's home. We could hear fighting in the distance but were so happy to be free and together that we did not even care about the uncertainty of the future.

Our journey away from the Khmer Rouge was dangerous, and there were many occasions when I thought we would not survive. Food was scarce, and there were still pockets of Khmer Rouge controlling our movements. We traveled with my cousin's family, who graciously shared the little food they had. We felt slightly better since our larger numbers gave us a feeling of increased security from our former captors, who still attacked during the nights.

It was a confusing time, and we were unsure of whose orders we should follow and how to survive. During our time in the camps, we knew the Khmer Rouge and those who they appointed were our enemies, and we might survive if we could prove our worth to them. During the panic and chaos caused by the Vietnamese approach, we did not really know who the enemy was anymore.

We were told the Vietnamese would kill us, but we also heard stories of newcomers being executed by the Khmer Rouge as their last chance to finish the extermination that started almost four years earlier. We moved as slowly as we could to give the illusion of cooperation with the Khmer Rouge, so they would not kill us while still distancing ourselves as much as possible from them. There was no doubt in our minds that the Khmer Rouge would still kill us if they were given the chance.

During the nights, my cousin's husband and Mom would search for enough food to sustain us for the next day. This was particularly dangerous because the Khmer Rouge laid explosive traps around some of the compounds that housed the rice, and there were many people killed by the explosives.

Many deaths ensued from the hand-to-hand combat that accompanied the nightly search for food. Thousands of starving people trying to gather food for themselves and their families inevitably led to fighting and death. It was an animal-like time where only the strongest survived.

Though my mom was not particularly strong or skilled in fighting, the suffering she endured under the barbaric Khmer Rouge and those Cambodians they empowered gave her the experience she needed to sneak around the fighting and successfully keep our family alive.

After three weeks of hiding, fear, and more than a few close encounters, we were told the Vietnamese successfully conquered the village of Angchot, and we could safely return. For the first time in almost four years, we were truly free from enslavement by the Khmer Rouge!

We returned to Angchot and moved into the house that belonged to my grandparents before the Khmer Rouge. The house was used as the Khmer Rouge's version of a hospital during the occupation where people went to die when they were unable to work anymore. We were uncomfortable since we all felt the spirits of those who suffered and died there remained, but we were still grateful and determined to make the most of our second chance at life.

"When we give cheerfully and accept gratefully, everyone is blessed." ~Maya Angelou

Chapter 8
Thumbprints

The catastrophic social experiment that tried to force Cambodia back in time to an agrarian society resulted in a nation that was simply unable to join modern society again. The few hundred thousand survivors of the forced evacuation of Phnom Penh were mostly widows and children who were traumatized and suffered from many different ailments caused by their four-year deprivation at the hands of the Khmer Rouge.

Many of the other surviving Cambodians were brainwashed and dejected peasant villagers, who also suffered greatly during the Khmer Rouge occupation. There were almost no professionals or skilled workers, and the few professionals who survived the genocide were understandably anxious to leave the country.

The years following our liberation were
spent under strict communist rule. Farmland
was divided according to the size of the
family, and like most of the people who
were called newcomers, at first, we were just
happy to enjoy the chance to live together
as a family whose lives were not constantly
threatened.

Unfortunately, the four years of psychological games and torture took its toll on
most people, and there was almost no trust
among Cambodians. The deception and
treachery of the Khmer Rouge were evident
in the paranoia and mistrust among neighbors and within families.

The years of abuse we endured under
the Khmer Rouge left more than psychological injuries. My mom began to suffer
enormous pain in her left leg that had
become severely infected and left untreated
for months during the last year of the Pol
Pot reign. As days passed, the pain left Mom
hardly able to walk, and the condition
showed little signs of improvement.

Inquiries among the villages told Mom
her best chance for improving her condition
was a healer who lived near the Vietnamese
border. I went with Mom, and we traveled

by ox-cart for almost three days to reach the medicine man, whose treatment eventually did heal my mom's leg and allowed her to walk again.

We returned to the village three weeks later to learn that my mom was going to be arrested for treason. Someone in the village reported my mom to the Vietnamese authority for meeting with Prince Sihanouk during the time we spent with the medicine man.

The treachery and mistrust that caused so much death during the Khmer Rouge's occupation continued long after our liberation. I suppose it should not have been surprising that people who had lost their entire families would try to seek vengeance against somebody they perceived as luckier than them or something even more sinister. Mom did not know exactly who made the false accusation, but it was common knowledge that many people resented her status as the vegetable grower for the village during the Khmer Rouge occupation since she was able to sustain herself and her family better than many others.

The absurdity of the accusation of a sick and traumatized widow, who had endured four years as one of the Khmer Rouge's

millions of slave laborers, somehow connecting with the ousted Prince Sihanouk to
overthrow the Vietnamese government likely
saved my mom from immediate execution.
Nonetheless, Mom was arrested and jailed in
a cell approximately twelve kilometers away.

My brother and I were devastated. After
the pain of being separated and captive for
so long, it just did not seem fair that we
were destined to be apart again. Rick was so
horrified by Mom's arrest that he could not
even bring himself to visit her in prison. The
occupation had taken its toll on him, and he
was simply unable to bear the pain of seeing
our mom in a jail cell.

I could not bear to be away from Mom
no matter where she was. As soon as I was
allowed to visit, I wrapped some rice and
fish in a banana leaf and set out to see her.
Thoughts of the dangers I might encounter
traveling alone or the discomfort of such a
long journey without shoes did not occur to
me, and my mom's weeping when she saw
me approaching her cell surprised me.

We embraced with the same loving support we shared during our time as prisoners
of the Khmer Rouge, and I reminded Mom
of the decision I made when I ran away from

my labor group for the last time. Home was where Mom was, and we would be together or we would die trying. We drew strength from each other, and our love strengthened our faith that everything would somehow be okay.

Amazingly, things were better than okay. After several more visits over a few weeks, my mom was released. By the grace of God and the goodness of many of the villagers, Mom was spared, and all charges against her were dropped.

There were definitely people who harbored a lot of misplaced resentment toward my mom, even though she lost her husband and suffered greatly, too. These were the people who accused Mom of treason. Despite all the treachery, my mom's inner strength and poise of character were evident, as she never uttered an unkind word about those people.

Then there were the villagers whose belief in Mom's strength of character saved her from execution or a lifetime in prison. Those villagers whose mind had not been poisoned by the Khmer Rouge or their own bitterness knew my mom and knew that she was honest, hardworking, and kind-hearted.

Those brave villagers took the unprecedented step of starting a petition for her release.

The people convinced one of the few people in the village who was literate to draft a letter stating that Mom was innocent of the crime of treason and should be released immediately. Such action had never been taken before, and the majority of people were not able to write an X, never mind signing their names.

The villagers decided to make their mark and stand by my mom using their thumbprint. Less than a month after she was imprisoned, Mom was released because almost every man, woman, and child in the newly liberated village of Angchot staked their lives on her innocence by way of a thumbprint.

"Sometimes the strength of motherhood is greater than natural laws."
~Barbara Kingsolver

Chapter 9
Mom's Strength

Pol Pot's democratic Kampuchea made all knowledge of the past illegal and anything designed to bring pleasure into life was abolished. There were no cars, families, music, stores, hospitals, post offices, infrastructure or factories. There was nothing to make life easier.

This resulted in a newly liberated nation with no buttons, zippers, books, plastic or anything else that was produced mechanically. After four years in the now-deserted labor camps, our clothes were tattered rags. When the Vietnamese invaded, we left with a single pot of shrimp paste as our only possession, and most newcomers left with little more than us. Cambodians were desperate for the most basic supplies, all of which came illegally from neighboring Thailand or Vietnam.

When most people hear the word smuggling, they think about illegal drugs or other substances that are banned for whatever reason. For me, smuggling makes me think of opportunity and survival.

My mom's resourcefulness saved our lives many times during the four years we spent in camps as slaves belonging to the Khmer Rouge. The gold Mom packed from our home in Phnom Penh bought her two life-saving capsules of penicillin that saved my brother's leg from a ravaging infection that was poisoning him. Her ability to combine ingredients to substitute for those not available at the camps earned her an unofficial and coveted spot in the kitchen. My mother never let an apparently hopeless situation make her feel hopeless.

Before the fall of Cambodia, we enjoyed a very comfortable life by Western standards and a life of luxury by Cambodian standards. Mom was determined to give us the best possible life after our liberation and knew that there were greater opportunities than simply farming our designated plot of land. Though the highest standard of living in the new Cambodia was lower than she had ever experienced prior to the occupation, Mom would not settle for anything less than the best for Rick and me.

Mom saw the need for the most basic supplies in Cambodia and recognized the opportunity to earn money from buying goods from the Thai border and selling them at a small profit to people in Phnom Penh. There was an entire city of people with no manufactured goods and nobody to buy them from. Mom knew she would help her fellow Cambodians by bringing them the supplies they desperately needed and help our family by building the capital she needed to start her own business and provide a life that was closer to the one we'd previously enjoyed.

There were two trains that carried government supplies that almost connected Cambodia to Thailand. Though trading was illegal, and the Vietnamese would occasionally arrest traders as a token reminder, it was necessary and widely accepted. The few that were caught were never punished.

The conductors of the trains would permit people smugglings goods from neighboring Thailand to ride on the top of the train for a fee. This was common practice, and my mom was able to leave Angchot, get her supplies from the traders at the Thai border, sell the goods in Phnom Penh, and be back in Angchot in one week.

Though I understood Mom was trying to provide us with some financial security, I suffered from terrible anxiety while she was gone. There were still more than one hundred thousand active Khmer Rouge soldiers in the jungle, and they often raided various supply convoys.

My mom successfully traded the goods from the Thai border for a few months when she was on a trip and had a close brush with death. The Khmer Rouge hijacked the other train and slaughtered the people who were on board. As Mom's train drove past the field where more than five hundred bodies lay, she was overwhelmed by thoughts of how easily she could have been on that train and left my brother and me orphans. Mom decided that it was not worth the risk and vowed to earn a good living and support her family some other way.

At the same time, news of the massacre reached our village, and I was overwhelmed by dread. I knew that Mom was in the area on a buying trip and would be heading home around that time. There was no way for me to find out if Mom was on the train that was hijacked or the other one. It took three days for her to get home, and I remember pacing the roads, squinting to see her shape in the distance all the while hoping and praying for her safe return.

Mom arrived safely, and it was cause for celebration. Neighbors told Mom she had a guardian angel looking out for her, and we did not disagree. It had been too much for me to bear this time, and I begged my mom not to return to the border. I reminded her that nothing was worth her safety.

Thankfully, Mom had seen the aftermath of the attack on the other train and had already decided to stop trading goods. Two weeks after the train hijacking, Mom decided that she was strong and resourceful enough to earn a good living in the city, and she left for Phnom Penh to find a place for us to live.

I missed my mom and was tormented and harassed by neighbors and family alike when Mom left for Phnom Penh. My paternal grandmother and aunt, who accepted their new lives as pheasant farmers, enjoyed calling me the "daughter of a whore" and spreading rumors among the villagers about my mom's whereabouts.

After four years of physical and psychological abuse by the Khmer Rouge, my grandma's spirit was broken, and she was unable to talk about anything other than the loss she endured during the genocide and how it had ruined and continued to ruin her life. Sadly, she died more than twenty years after the liberation without ever really experiencing freedom. Grandma lived in a prison of her own fashioning and expected everyone else to remain as tortured as she was.

Despite the rumors that must have been so painful for my mom, who remained faithful to my father's memory to this day, Mom made every visit to the village as exciting as Christmas during the six months she was in Phnom Penh without us. The visits were always around religious holidays that were especially important in 1979 because religion was banned for the duration of the Pol Pot regime.

Rick stayed with an aunt in another village while Mom was gone, so he would be able to travel the distance to where the high-school level classes were offered. I always knew an approximate day for my mom's arrival, and even though I had tremendous household responsibilities keeping our house and farming the rice for Rick, Grandma, and me, I would always position myself so I could see her approaching long before she actually arrived in our home.

Mom's visits began with hugs, laughter, comfort and the release of any misgiving I had about her absence. We were always so grateful to be reunited that our love melted away all tensions caused by our separation.

Mom brought presents from the city, too: flip-flops and a new T-shirt and sarong were the gifts from one visit. I still remember ber the pride I felt when I attended the ceremony at the temple as the best-dressed girl in the village next to the best-dressed mother. They were simple gifts by today's standards, but the gift of a flashlight in a village without electricity was spectacular.

Mom's visits from the city brought me more than a comforting cuddle and some items that made me more comfortable. Mom knew what people said about her and understood that her family had started the rumors. Despite this, she remained poised and gracious. Mom would bring gifts to the very people who tormented her, and, in doing so, taught me one of the most valuable lessons I have learned in life: it is not your business what anybody else thinks of you. Do your best, and your best will be enough.

"There was never a good war or a bad peace." ~Benjamin Franklin

Chapter 10
Back to Phnom Penh

Once called The Pearl of Asia, Phnom Penh was one of the most beautiful French colonial cities in Southeast Asia. The city boasted a thriving multicultural market, the stunning Olympic Stadium, and was considered the gateway to the world's largest religious monument: Angkor Wat.

After the Khmer Rouge forced all inhabitants from the city on April 17, 1975, it remained deserted until the liberation in 1979. The neglect was evident throughout the great city, and there was little evidence of the city's former beauty. Though intact, Phnom Penh was thoroughly looted and in complete disrepair. Western journalists often compared the city to an eerie movie set without actors. The stench from the malfunctioning sewer system was overwhelming, and there were even piles of worthless money lying in the gutters.

Many of the bridges and roads were impassable, and the mazes of exposed wire throughout the city claimed many lives, every single day. The Khmer Rouge executed virtually every engineer, city planner, electrician, and anybody else who might come to Phnom Penh's aid to restore the city to even a fraction of its former glory.

Despite the hazardous state of Phnom Penh, within weeks of our liberation, its population swelled from almost zero to more than one hundred thousand refugees. In the chaos and lawlessness that ensued, it is amazing that there were not more deaths.

Since the Khmer Rouge murdered most of the past city dwellers, the new population of the city was largely peasant farmers who were accustomed to a very different lifestyle, where their homes were more distant from each other and there was significantly less contact with others. Communicable diseases ravaged the heavier populated areas, and with no medicine or access to clean water, the ever-increasing population of Phnom Penh was in grave danger.

The Khmer Rouge destroyed all government documents, books, and records they found in 1979. Not that it would have mattered. Similar to what is now called squatter's rights, people took up residence wherever they chose as long as they got permission from the Vietnamese authority. When somebody found a vacant apartment, they would seek permission from the authority to occupy the flat, pay whatever fee the individual in charge of the area requested, and claim it as their own. Most of the actual owners were dead since only a small fraction of the city's former residents survived the genocide.

After my mom had established her rice trading business in Phnom Penh, she brought Rick and me to Phnom Penh to live. Mom, Rick, and me were one of the twenty families who were governed by a Vietnamese appointed leader who was Cambodian. We had to report each other's behavior to the group leader similar to when we reported to the Khmer Rouge appointed leader who was Cambodian when we were in Angchot. Though they liberated us from the Khmer Rouge, the Vietnamese were strictly communist, and their law was not taken lightly. However, unlike the Khmer Rouge and the vengeful Cambodians they appointed, the Vietnamese took no pleasure in our punishment, and we were not penalized for a lack of transgressions to report.

Like most communist societies, corruption was rampant, and there was always an official with his hand ready to receive a bribe in exchange for his approval. Mom had to bribe the Vietnamese authority for permission to move into our apartment and to ensure her rice business would be permitted to grow. There were the legal and government-imposed taxes and expenses that accompanied real estate and business transactions, but Mom always needed additional cash to pay directly to many different individuals in our years in Phnom Penh. It was a happy time despite the drastically different standard of living from the lifestyle we enjoyed before the occupation. As soon as we were settled, Rick and I began attending school for the second time in our lives, in Phnom Penh.

The new school was very different from the private school we attended in the days before the fall of Cambodia. Our new school was a recreation center that the Vietnamese converted into a school. There were no toilets for the students, and my mind will always see the pool filled with water so full of algae that it resembled green slime as though it were yesterday even though decades have passed. The navy tunics with school crests and white blouses from my past school would have been outrageous in this school.

It was a very difficult time for the teacher and the students. During the Khmer Rouge regime, everybody suffered to varying extents, and this was reflected in the students. Emotional scarring and post-traumatic stress affected almost everybody's performance. Supplies were inadequate, and the teacher was very limited in the material he was permitted to teach.

There were many children in the new school whose losses were far greater than mine. I became good friends with a girl whose indescribable beauty was the only reason she was not executed with her parents. We enjoyed learning and playing together like most school-aged children, and one might never have believed what we had endured from appearance alone.

Sadly, outside appearances seldom reflect one's inner experience, and my dear friend was no exception. She had been traumatized by the murder of her family and practically raising herself from the age of twelve, and life was continually unkind to her. My friend was alone in the world and, not surprisingly, measured her worth by her appearance. When I returned to Cambodia for the first time in 1994, I tracked her down and was dismayed to learn that she earned her living as a kind of mistress. There was little joy in her life, and she told me she was just waiting to join her parents.

Nonetheless, Rick and I were determined to make the most of the education that was available to us. Our dad always emphasized the importance of a good education, and we tried to honor him by doing our best. We both did very well in our classes despite the lack of proper facilities and supplies. I remember feeling lucky to have a friend who lived nearby, so I could use her bathroom if I was unable to contain myself during school hours. As a child who had lived in Year Zero for four years, attending a school without a toilet was no big deal to me.

In the evenings, we helped Mom prepare for her day at the rice stand. I loved the time we spent in the evenings helping Mom prepare for the next day's work: we were working together for something that was going to help our family. Mom's rice stall thrived in the first few months in Phnom Penh. My mom was honest, hardworking, and always had a smile and a kind word to give to every customer. Her stall was opened early and stayed open late. She also equipped her stall with a few other items she thought her customers might need. It was only natural that people gravitated to Mom's stall, and she did very well.

Rick and I also excelled in our schooling. There were loose standards for admittance from one level to the next, but we both wrote the examinations with ease. We recognized that we had lost more than four years of our education, and we wanted to make up for the lost time.

Our life in Phnom Penh was becoming better and better until the day the headmaster told Rick he had to leave school. He said Rick had to offer his seat to the much younger children with no education.

Rick was very disappointed but always carried himself with remarkable dignity and agreed with the headmaster, shook his hand, and wished him well in his noble mission to educate Cambodia's youth. I could see the pain in my brother's eyes as he spoke the words, but my heart swelled with pride since I knew he was exercising the diplomacy my dad was known for.

When I arrived home after school, I could tell Rick had been crying, but I didn't ask and he did not share his feelings. His mission was to build an empire from Mom's rice stand. I was so very proud of him and secretly wondered if I would have been able to exercise the same diplomacy my brother had shown.

Mom was very unhappy to hear that there was no position for Rick in school, but like Rick, she only chose to see the good and declared that with two great people working the stand, we could not help but succeed!

The rice stand was extremely successful. Mom and Rick would put their very best into serving their customers, and their return was more than adequate to fill our little family's needs. I studied hard at school and achieved phenomenal scores. We were so happy and on our way to the new life we dreamed of when Rick received the news that changed everything: Rick was conscripted to join the Cambodian military.

For the very first time, I saw my mom break down. We lost our home, my father, our way of life and our dignity, and she did not break down like she did that day. "Enough!" she said. "No more fighting. This family has had enough fighting!!"

Those words sent Rick on his own journey and Mom and me on our journey that took four years to complete. Rick left Phnom Penh soon after to head for Thailand. Mom was subjected to many harsh Vietnamese interrogations about his whereabouts, but she denied any knowledge of his fleeing Cambodia.

Those few years in Phnom Penh were the only normal childhood that I had besides my very young years before the Khmer Rouge. Once Mom and I fled Phnom Penh, life was lawless and chaotic once more.

"Everything you want is on the other side of fear." ~Jack Canfield

Chapter 11
Zipper Trees

Once we left Phnom Penh, it was virtually impossible to distinguish friends from enemies. The Vietnamese liberators who saved our lives became our new tormentors. Anyone caught fleeing Cambodia was executed for treason against the new government. There were large pockets of active Khmer Rouge still trying to complete their unfinished mission, and there were other Khmer Rouge soldiers who were trying to flee Cambodia who would also kill us so they could steal our goods. Even the smugglers on the bus with us posed a threat to our safety since we had no protectors and nowhere to hide our belongings. Enemies were everywhere.

Our escape from Cambodia to the refugee camp in Thailand took more than

three months. Nothing I experienced in the
four years I spent in slave labor could have
prepared me for the danger and horror of
the Cambodian jungle. The lawlessness in
and around the villages and cities after the
Vietnamese liberation was not even comparable to the chaos that ruled deep in the
Cambodian jungle.

As the bus drove away from the city into
the countryside, my feelings of sadness and
loss quickly changed into an overwhelming
feeling I can only describe as sickeningly
uncomfortable. Memories and thoughts of
the beatings and murders of newcomers who
identified themselves as professionals in the
days before the Khmer Rouge; the children
and elderly who were not deemed useful
enough to live and were slaughtered; the
beautiful woman whose smooth hands indi-
cated that she had enjoyed a pampered life at
the expense of the peasant who was dragged
away and never seen again. I thought about
my father and wondered how frightened
he had been just before he was killed. Was
he thinking of me when the Khmer Rouge
killed him? These and other thoughts raced
through my mind as Phnom Penh faded into
the distance. This countryside had seen more

than a million murders, and I found myself feeling smothered by the road that led to the jungle.

Sensing my unease, my mom discreetly stroked my hand with her gentle and soothing way, and I heard my father's voice, "Keep moving, Pisey. Look away and everything will be okay." My mom's gentle touch combined with my dad's urgent yet soothing voice from my memory allowed me to center myself and focus on convincingly portraying a smuggler. Mom's experience smuggling goods from the Thai border to Phnom Penh helped us play this role more convincingly. Mom knew the lingo and the routes, so it was easy to deceive people into thinking smuggling was our intention.

There were several checkpoints where I was certain we were going to be killed. At one point, I was questioned, and I remember being terrified for my life. The Vietnamese accused me of trying to defect and threatened to kill me. Somehow I remained poised and seemingly unnerved, and I was released back to the group where my mom looked like she was on the verge of collapse.

As we started to move past the checkpoint, Mom warned me that if she was detained, I should get to the Thai border without her. Mom received a letter from Rick just before we left telling her he arrived safely. Mom knew my only chance of survival without her would be if I could get to Rick. I started to protest and tell Mom that I would stay with her no matter what happened and was silenced by a look I dared not question. My mom said simply, "You will get to Thailand, with or without me." I knew from the time Rick left, we would not be able to turn back on our plan, but I had never considered what might happen if Mom was killed. The frightening thought of finding my way through the jungle alone terrified me and caused me to pray for our safe passage with even more intensity.

We left the slight feeling of security the bus provided at its last stop in the Western city of Battambang and started the most dangerous part of our journey—approximately one hundred miles of harsh jungle filled with three different military camps fighting against the Vietnamese and each other. The jungle and countryside were also littered with land mines planted by the Khmer Rouge as they retreated from the Vietnamese.

There was a coalition formed to overthrow the Vietnamese government comprised of three unlikely allies: the Khmer Rouge, General Son Sann's Khmer People's National Liberation Front, and Prince Sihanouk's Coalition Government of Democratic Kampuchea. This coalition was called the Coalition Government of Democratic Kampuchea and was supported by Western superpowers and China. Though few wanted the Khmer Rouge to rule Cambodia, chances of a government formed without the support of the Khmer Rouge overthrowing the Vietnamese were slim. Fighting among the three groups in the coalition was regular and ultimately caused its demise after several years.

Mom understood the danger we faced and decided to leave me with a cousin while she scouted out the best route for us and secured the services of a guide she trusted. Many thousands of people died trying to escape Cambodia, and Mom was determined to keep us alive. We walked together for a few days into the jungle when we arrived at Son Sann's camp where my cousin was based. Mom arranged for me to stay while she left to find the safest route for us to escape to Thailand.

Saying goodbye to Mom was excruciating. Though she assured me she would return as quickly as she could, we both knew the risks were extremely high and that not many others had successfully navigated through the jungle she would travel. Time passed very slowly as I awaited Mom's return, and when she finally arrived, I was overwhelmed with joy.

Mom told me it was much worse than she thought, but she found a route and a guide she trusted who would lead us to freedom. The next morning, we said goodbye to our family, left the camp, and moved toward the border. As we walked away from the camp, I wondered if we would ever see our family again.

The ever-thickening jungle became more challenging to navigate within minutes of leaving the camp. Within an hour, the light that filtered through the thick trees was so dim that it seemed more like dusk than noon. The air was moist and heavy, and everything was covered in green. Even the rocks were covered in moss, and the jungle began to feel like a living and merciless creature that was determined to halt our progress.

The path our guide led us on was narrow but well used. Since the Khmer Rouge planted land mines everywhere, we dared not deviate from the trail. The trail had ruts from the wagons and bicycles that traveled before us, and the mud was deep along the trails. The unforgiving bamboo roots that lay hidden in the mud tormented Mom greatly and put her at risk of slipping and falling away from the path and landing on a mine. I was so light that I did not sink far enough into the mud to feel the roots, and our guide wore soccer cleats, but Mom was not as lucky. The roots were slimy, and Mom was forced to dig her toenails into the roots in order to keep from falling. About a week after we arrived at the refugee camp, those toenails that helped Mom stay on the path became infected and fell off.

We trudged through the afternoon, and I was growing weary when a beautiful sight caught my attention on the trail ahead. It was a tree with blooms of shiny silver, and I pointed to it and said, "Look, Mom, look at that tree ahead!" I hurried off the path toward the tree when our guide's shout sent shivers up my spine and caused me to freeze. Seconds felt like hours after the guide ordered me not to move a muscle. He stepped gingerly in my footprints until he reached me and carried me back to the safety of the trail. The blooms on the tree were zippers that exploded into the air and landed on the tree when the smuggler who carried them detonated a land mine to the left of the trail.

We were all more than a little shaken as we silently walked past the tree and tried not to think about how close I had come to ending our journey. The guide suggested we walk in a single file and step in his footprints. It was slow going, but within an hour we saw the makeshift Buddhist temple near the border where we planned to rest for the night before our escape into Thailand in the morning.

The temple looked like a small piece of heaven to me as I wearily walked toward the entrance. Buddhist nuns appeared and welcomed us into the temple for the night. We slept in the huts where the nuns slept and spent the next day in hiding. When the evening came, and we had the cover of darkness, the nuns blessed us with sacred earth and asked God to protect us as we crossed the border. It was only a short distance to the border, but many before us had made it this far and not reached their destination.

As we got closer to the border, I could hear shouting, gunfire, and crying. I knew somebody had been injured or killed, and I was terrified. I wondered if we would make it or if we would be the next to die. The guide explained earlier that we needed to lie flat on the ground until he gave the signal. As I lay on the ground squeezing Mom's hand, I prayed like never before. "Please let us through. I don't want to die." Over and over, I repeated the prayer until I saw the guide indicate it was time to run.

We leapt up from the ground and started running toward the border. The Thai army built a dirt wall to prevent people from crossing, but we ran up and over it and landed with a hard thud on the Thai side of the border. Without even a moment to catch our breath, the guide hurried us into the bushes where we began the three-mile trek to Khao-I-Dang holding camp.

We crept through the thick jungle until we arrived near the gates of the refugee camp and lay in the brush to wait until the water truck drove into camp at dawn, and the gates would open. The area around the gate was patrolled for refugees, and we were exposed for the entire sprint from the bushes to the entrance.

We heard the sound of the truck approaching, and the gates began to open. We jumped up from the bushes and were immediately spotted by a Thai soldier. Unbeknown to us, our guide bribed the Thai guard on our behalf and ran toward us with his rifle pointed far too high to hit us and began shouting. I did not know he was not going to kill us, and I froze in shock and terror.

"GO, GO, GO! Run through the gate!" our guide shouted. On one side of me, I saw my mom trip on some barbed wire. I turned to the other side and saw Cambodians workers inside the camp gates yelling for us and gesturing for us to run. It was like a dream or a slow-motion sequence in a movie. I took a deep breath and ran as fast as I could toward the gate. I glanced behind and saw Mom running too, and we ran until we reached the arms of the workers and collapsed.

I remember crying as they carried us away and into hiding in a hut. The rest is a blur. We made it out of the jungle, but our journey was far from complete. Though the UN workers refused to turn any refugee away from the camp, the Thai government had declared the camp full and set up a task force specifically designed to separate the registered refugees from the new refugees like us. Unregistered refugees found by the task force were transported back to the border where most were killed.

"There is no easy walk to freedom anywhere, and many of us will have to pass through the valley of the shadow of death again and again before we reach the mountaintop of our desires." ~Nelson Mandela

Chapter 12
A Year in a Chicken Cage

Life under the Khmer Rouge was comparable to life in a prison without walls. There were no rooms with bars or locks to keep us from coming and going. We moved freely to and from our work as a group with little interference from the Khmer Rouge.

Of course, any transgression from the expected behavior resulted in severe punishment or death, but that was one of the Angkar's ways of brainwashing us. If we were punished, it was because we chose to do something that deviated from what the Angkar expected.

During those four years, I could not imagine a fate worse than that which we endured every day: the spying and prying eyes of privileged villagers waiting for the opportunity to find fault with us and the vicious guards who were too eager to punish. It was a horrific experience that I knew I was lucky to survive.

When we arrived at Khao-I-Dang holding center one week after they officially stopped allowing more refugees in, I realized that there were fates much worse than the life I had endured under the Khmer Rouge. Life as an illegal refugee was much worse than life under the Khmer Rouge.

By the time I made it to Khao-I-Dang, I had more life experiences I would prefer to forget than those I would prefer to remember. Other than a few cherished memories of my young life before the fall of Cambodia when I was only seven, I played many unenviable roles. I was an expendable slave laborer for the Khmer Rouge, who measured my worth by my capacity to plant rice or pick up cow manure. The labor camps were like prisons without walls. Our prison bars were the prying and spying eyes of other Cambodians who hoped to gain favor with the Khmer Rouge by reporting our so-called crimes.

After the liberation, I was the tormented daughter of a jailed criminal who was accused of plotting to overthrow the

Vietnamese government. In Phnom Penh, I was a student in a school without toilets who lived in an apartment without running water or reliable electricity. There were no murderous guards willing me to make a mistake, so they could have the privilege of killing me, but the communist Vietnamese and their appointed spies were always watching, and minor transgressions against their party were not tolerated. Though there were no prison bars or guards, every aspect of our life was controlled and monitored by the government.

On my journey to the refugee camp, I was a teenager stepping around land mines and running through the jungle with armed men chasing me. When I finally reached my destination and sanctuary, global politics worked against me, and I became an illegal refugee hiding in a hole in the ground covered by a chicken cage. For the first time in my life, I was physically restrained. I spent countless hours hiding in a dirt hole. I was hunted in the evening by the raiding bandits who captured many young women and took them away to keep as their wives. The Thai task force spent the mornings searching the huts for unregistered refugees to send back to the jungle.

For most of my memory, I was oppressed and afraid of somebody. Khao-I-Dang holding facility brought that oppression and fear to an entirely different level. I could not have imagined a life worse than the life I lead under the Khmer Rouge, but I was mistaken. The raiding bandits from the camps of General Son Sinn and Prince Sihanouk were ruthless and merciless. Every night we tried to sleep close to the hospital since they avoided the guarded areas.

There was an unsophisticated but effective public address system that would alert the refugees about the evening's raid. The megaphones mounted on poles would sound the alarm and announce the location of the pending attack, and people would scatter and flee the area.

The system worked well for us until one night the bandits were too close before the announcement for us to flee to a different area of the camp. We heard the soldiers approaching our hut, and we began to panic.

"What are we going to do, Mom?" I asked. There was no time to think and nowhere to go. In a quick gesture of the ultimate sacrifice, Mom shoved Rick and me into the hole and placed the chicken cage on top just in time to turn and face the bandit who entered our hut.

He began shouting at Mom to give him her gold. Mom pleaded that she did not have any gold, and he drew his gun and pointed it at her head. Rick and I were mere inches away and could hear my mom's breath become shallow and rapid as the intensity of the situation increased.

"I am a woman who escaped alone!" Mom cried "I do not have any gold left. I used it all to get here." The soldier was unmoved, and we were sure he was going to kill Mom when she reached to her right, grabbed the small tin that contained a few coins, and shook it in his direction. "Here, it's all I have left," she said. "It's yours. Please take it."

I never figured out if it was the rattle of the coins in such sharp contrast to Mom's gentle pleading or if the soldier just took pity on a desperate lady, but he lowered his gun and said, "I don't want your coins. The noise will get me killed in the jungle. Listen to this!" He rustled his pants to the answering sound of rattling coins. "I don't want these either!" He said, "Take them for yourself!"

To our complete astonishment, the bandit tossed the coins on the floor in front of Mom, threw his hands up in exasperation, and stormed out of our hut. There was silence as we each wondered if he would return with his gun. A few minutes passed with no sign of the soldier. After a few more minutes had elapsed, it was evident by the silence surrounding our hut that the bandits had retreated, and we were safe.

Rick and I scrambled out of the hole into Mom's arms where we all held each other in amazement and delight. Adrenalin rushed through my body, and I began to cry In all we'd experienced, it was the closest I came to losing Mom, and it was more than a few minutes before my sobs diminished into hiccups.

We never experienced another close call like that again. During the nights, we slept by the hospital and sneaked back into our hole beneath the chicken cage before the Thai task force would start their morning search for illegal refugees. We spoke to a woman and her child who were illegal and got taken away and made it back a second time.

Before the conversation with the woman, we had no idea what happened to the illegal refugees who were caught. We saw them on the back of the truck and knew they were driven away, but that was all we knew. The woman told us they drove them close to the Thai border and forced them off the truck and drove away. The woman said it was like they were bags of trash and not human beings.

I knew from experience how dangerous the journey from the border to the camp was and asked the woman how she and her child could possibly have been lucky enough to make it twice. She replied that God was her guide.

A few weeks after my conversation with that woman, the UN opened the camp for the illegal refugees to register. Mom and I were finally permitted to stay and had rations of our own to eat. It was truly amazing. After many years of struggling to survive, we knew we were safe. There were food, shelter, and hope for a life of freedom.

"I would like to be remembered as a person who wanted to be free so other people would be also free." ~Rosa Parks

Chapter 13
Leaving Asia

Time passed quickly in Khao-I-Dang once we finally registered with the UN. The camp was still dangerous, but the raids became less frequent. I threw myself into studying and registered for almost every course the camp offered. I knew that speaking English would increase my chances of being accepted into a new country, and I wanted to make the time pass as quickly as possible.

The English lessons offered by the camp cost two baht per lesson. I seldom had the money for lessons, so I learned most of my first English vocabulary from the missionaries who taught Bible classes. Those classes were free.

I also enrolled in courses that trained me to work in public health. The population of the camp was largely Khmer Rouge, who lived most of their lives in a rural or jungle setting and were unequipped to handle life in a crowded refugee camp where communicable diseases were rampant.

My first job was visiting huts and distributing and applying cream to treat scabies. This highly contagious skin disease tormented almost everybody in the camp. I will always remember the poor children of Khmer Rouge peasants, whose broken limbs were in plaster casts. Their lack of experience and instruction in hygiene, coupled with the scabies epidemic, left their little limbs festering and excruciatingly painful beneath their casts. The parents were often unaware or indifferent to the treatment that was readily available and necessary to help the children, so I brought treatment to them.

My work in public health paid me in rations of cigarettes that I sold for money to pay for my English lessons. While working with the public health division, I enrolled in more medical training and eventually I became a full-time physician's assistant working in the camp's hospital. An American-trained doctor always checked my diagnoses, but my opinion was respected, and my position was a source of pride.

Things were going well for my family. I was immersed in English all day at the hospital and studying during the evenings, so I was making great progress when we received a letter from the aunt who hid Mom and me under her hut when we first arrived at Khao-I-Dang. My aunt, and her five children were thriving in New Zealand and wondered if we would like her sponsorship.

My heart soared as I read the news to Mom. I eagerly responded that we would be so grateful for the opportunity to live in New Zealand and would she please start the process as quickly as she was able. Mom and I spent the evening sharing our hopes and dreams about what our life would be like if we were accepted to New Zealand.

Six months later, we were granted an interview with the representative from New Zealand where I explained the relationship between Mom and my auntie. A few days after the interview, we learned that we were accepted and would be going to New Zealand.

Words cannot express the joy and relief I felt when I learned we would have a home. The only time I remember being as happy and relieved was when I finally spied my mother amid the masses of people fleeing the Khmer Rouge's labor camp after the Vietnamese liberation when I was just ten years old. It was incredible.

There was a board at the front of the camp where people who were approved by host countries to leave the camp would see their names and get information about their travel times. As weeks of waiting turned into months with no sign of our names, our tension mounted, and I began to fear the worst. "What if they've changed their minds?" I asked Mom. "What if we don't find a new country and get sent back to Cambodia?" Repatriation was my biggest fear since there were whispers among staff at the hospital that the refugee camps would close soon.

Three months after our acceptance to New Zealand, I received a letter from my friend who was in the Phanat Nikhom holding facility saying how pleased he was to see our names on the list of future arrivals and telling us he would see us next week.

"Next week?" I thought to myself. "There are names of people listed on the board who are leaving in two months, and our names aren't even listed yet. He must be mistaken." It turned out my friend was right,

119

and our names were added to our camp's board the next morning. Our tense and anxious wait turned into a flurry of goodbyes, promises to remember and stay in touch, to distribute our few possessions to friends that remained, and more than a few tears. Five days later, we boarded a bus that drove us out of Khao-I-Dang for the last time.

As we drove away from camp, I was struck by the almost forgotten feeling of sickening discomfort I felt as we rode the bus away from Phnom Penh four years earlier. I remembered how Mom and I crept through the jungle and spent the day hiding with the Buddhist nuns who blessed us with sacred earth. I remembered the zipper tree and how close I had come to getting us killed. Mostly, I remembered the terror of seeing the armed soldier chasing me as I entered the camp and collapsed into the waiting arms of the refugee that carried me to safety.

These memories ran through my mind as I silently thanked God for saving my family, and I promised I would make the most of this opportunity to start our new life in New Zealand. I glanced at my mom and our eyes met. I did not need to ask what

120

she thought as she smiled sadly and reached across her lap to pat my hand. We were leaving Dad behind, but we were also leaving the horrors and fear behind as we moved closer to our goal of freedom and a better life.

Our stay in Phanat Nikhom was brief and within a few short weeks, we were on a similar bus bound for Bangkok. The whirlwind that saw my family and I change from frightened refugees with no departure date in sight to the day we arrived in New Zealand was an unprecedented 27 days. I will never know what expedited the process so much, but whatever the reason, we were on our way to our new life, and we were excited!

Part Three

"Our doubts are traitors and make us lose the good we oft might win by fearing to attempt." ~William Shakespeare

Chapter 14
Smothering Freedom

Personal liberty is, without question, the single most important determining factor in the quality of your life. During the days of the Khmer Rouge's reign of terror, I lived without any control of my life. I could not choose what to eat and was denied food most of the time. I was forced to use mud and tree bark to make my clothes look as much like the required black uniform as I was able. I was told how to speak; words like sleep were illegal, and I had to address my mom as "Comrade." The misguided Angkar even tried to control my thoughts with their brainwashing.

Life under the Khmer Rouge is one of the most extreme examples of a lack of freedom in the twentieth century. If you were born in a Western society, you are very blessed. You have undoubtedly experienced hardship and faced adversity, but your basic right of freedom has likely never been denied, and that is a great blessing. The majority of people living today will never know the peace and privacy of such a life. They do not have the right to criticize their government without fear of persecution. They do not have the security of knowing there are laws to protect their rights even if they should break the law. Many cannot even choose their career or the person they marry.

When I first learned we were accepted to New Zealand, I was so excited about the possibility of personal freedom. But it had been so many years since I had the right to live my life in the manner I chose that I did not know how. I was only seven when the Khmer Rouge captured Cambodia, and I had never been truly free since then. Growing up under the Khmer Rouge and the communist Vietnamese government, left me completely inexperienced in the skills of decision-making, goal setting, and planning. Aside from these skills, I also lacked knowledge of how to fit into a Western society.

Smothering Freedom

On October 28, 1988, Mom, Rick, and I officially moved into my auntie's house in Hamilton. For the first time since I was seven years old, I was truly free. I had more than enough food and could choose whatever I wanted to eat. I had a choice of clothing donated by the church, and I could dress in whatever style I chose. I could bathe, sleep, go outside, read a book and do whatever I wanted, whenever I wanted.

It was terrifying! My mind could not handle all the new responsibility, and the decisions I constantly had to make began to trouble me. Moving from a life where almost everything was decided for me, whether I agreed with the decision or not, to a so-called normal life in my new country, where I was entirely responsible for the results of my choices, left me unable to distinguish between big, important decisions with serious consequence and little, unimportant choices that would not really affect much. Of course, logic would tell me the difference, but my mind was overwhelmed by the constant need to choose one thing or another.

My mind was full of chatter day in and day out. I started my torturous daily ritual of decision-making trying to decide what I should eat for breakfast while simultaneously trying to decide if I would go for a walk or read a book. I wondered if I should have a bath before I ate or after my walk. Would I have tea or hot water with lemon? Sounds pretty normal so far, right?

I started to question my judgment and second-guess my abilities and choices, and before long, I was in a complete mess. I had a very poor self-image and lacked confidence. I began to ask myself if I made the right decision or if another decision would have yielded a better result. Within weeks, I was driving myself crazy wondering how the wrong decisions I made in my life affected me and which decisions I could have made differently. I also fantasized about what could have been.

It was a game I played against myself and my life spiraled quickly out of control. I began to obsess about the past as well as the future. These doubts turned into worry, and I began to worry about the what-ifs in my life: What if people did not understand my English? What if they laughed at my mistakes? What if I could not find a job? What if Mom got sick? I had survived the worst genocide in the latter half of the twentieth century and escaped armed soldiers chasing me through a jungle filled with land mines, and I was worrying myself to death about what-ifs.

I knew I could not continue the vicious cycle of negative self-talk and worry, but I felt powerless to stop it. My thoughts became so dark that I began to contemplate suicide. I could not explain or understand why I could not control my thinking, but death seemed like a much better choice than a life constantly filled with worry, doubt, and anxiety.

My mom watched me struggle with my newfound freedom and was deeply troubled by her inability to comfort me. I tried to hide my inner turmoil from her, but Mom knew I was struggling. For the first time in my life, Mom could not rescue me and save me from the enemy. I was my own enemy and rescue could only come from within.

One morning as I considered how to commit suicide so I could finally silence the relentless nagging voices that tormented me day and night, I heard the voice that carried me through so many horrific moments for the last nine years speaking to me: "Keep moving and look away, Pisey," Dad said from my mind. "Keep moving and everything will be okay." What could it mean? That was the expression I used so many times to control myself and to keep myself from reacting when I was in immediate danger, but why did I hear it now?

Perhaps it was my mind's way of reminding me just to keep going. Maybe it actually was my dad's spirit speaking to me when I needed him. Regardless of why I heard the words, they made me stop and assess my thinking. I realized I could not possibly dishonor the millions of Cambodians who died under the Khmer Rouge by taking my life. I knew I owed it to my dad to make something of the miracle of my survival and to succeed and love and grow and find happiness.

I decided then and there I would be happy and enjoy a life that made the struggles of the past nine years worthwhile. I began to examine my life with a critical eye, not so I could see what was wrong with it but so I could focus on what was right.

This subtle shift in thinking got me on my way to a life that is nothing short of magnificent. I began by making the decision to be happy and to create my own dream life instead of waiting to see what happened. The results of that decision have been wonderful.

"Knowing others is intelligence; knowing yourself is true wisdom. Mastering others is strength; Mastering yourself is true power."
~Lao-Tzu

Chapter 15
Mastering and Loving Myself

I did not know it at the time but making a decision to find the good in every part of my life was the first and most important step toward enjoying a life of serenity, wealth, and happiness. I now know I was the cause of all my problems with my negative thinking, but back then, I did not know how to control the destructive thought patterns, and I did not understand that I was making myself sick with my toxic thinking.

After struggling with depression, anxiety, insomnia, debilitating migraine headaches and stress-induced stomach troubles for thirteen months, I knew I had to make a change. Without question, the most challenging part of my transformation was learning to love and master myself: physically, mentally and spiritually.

My body had endured many years of malnourishment and hardship along the journey to freedom, and I had not taken care of myself since we arrived in New Zealand. I had low self-esteem and a very poor self-image. I certainly did not feel worthy of love or admiration, and mastering my mind posed a great challenge. I was stuck in my negative thought patterns, and they had become my habitual way of thinking. I no longer believed myself worthy of the newfound freedom I experienced and actually felt like it was unfair that I survived the genocide when so many others who were more deserving did not.

Nonetheless, I had already taken that first and most difficult step of deciding to find peace and happiness, and I refused to let bad habits deter me from reaching my goal of a life filled with happiness, love, peace and prosperity. I decided the best way to stop the destructive thoughts would be to replace them with positive thoughts of what I wanted.

The first step I took toward my goal was deciding what I wanted. I knew my auntie and her five children arrived in New Zealand like we had: flat broke with all our meager possessions in a cardboard box and no real knowledge of the culture or the language. Less than three years later, my auntie was a proud homeowner. I thought to myself, "There you go, Pisey. If auntie can do it, then so can you." The goal setting and achieving a pattern, which has resulted in great success in my life, had begun.

Visualization became the healthy alternative to my morning ritual of obsessing over what choices and decisions I would face that day. Instead of bombarding myself with decisions from the moment I woke up, I decided to flood my mind with beautiful images of what I wanted immediately after I awoke by rising one-hour earlier than Mom and Rick to ensure privacy and spending the hour visualizing myself healthy, happy, and peaceful and in possession of the beautiful home I desired.

My imagination helped me through some difficult times during my days under the Khmer Rouge and in the refugee camp. There were times when I was so exhausted and hungry that I would not have been able to carry on without the comfort I had when I escaped to the refuge of my imagination. I decided to try and call on that mighty power again to help me find my way out of the new prison I inadvertently created for myself and into the home and peaceful life I desired.

At first, it was tremendously difficult. The chatter in my head became a shouting and angry voice that ridiculed me whenever I tried to see myself in my new state of calm and bliss. I would find myself thinking I was not worthy of anyone's love and affection. As I would try to tell myself I was beautiful the way I was, the shouting inner-voice would remind me of my less-than-perfect teeth or my skinny and scarred legs. When I pictured myself walking into my beautiful home, the voice would remind me that I needed money to buy a home, and since I couldn't speak English, nobody wanted to give me a job.

Despite the challenges and periods of doubt, I persisted, and the loud voices got softer. I began to believe the kind things I told myself: I WAS worthy of love and affection, and I DID deserve to enjoy excellent health and abundant energy. I began to

believe that I was capable of earning enough
money to buy a home.

As I gained control of my thoughts,
I realized that I could not give what I did
not have, and my lack of love for myself
was preventing me from receiving the love
that was all around me. I started to imagine
my heart as a bank account where I had to
deposit love before it would be available for
withdrawal. I then started visualizing myself
walking into a bank and making a deposit
and added that image to my daily imagination exercise.

Amazingly, the stomach troubles and
headaches subsided and my quality of life
increased. I began to enjoy increased calm
and more happiness. I looked forward to
the hour I spent visualizing my healthy and
happy self each morning, and my body
began to thrive on the healthy thoughts I
provided.

My morning visualization played a
vital part in helping me master my negative
and destructive thought patterns. The more
skilled I became at quieting the nagging
inner-voices during my visualization, the
easier it became to quiet them throughout

the day. Before too long, I was able to stop negative and destructive thoughts simultaneously and turn them into positive thoughts throughout my day.

It was not easy, but I forced myself to replace every negative thought with a positive thought until it became a habit. At first, it felt like a lie and really, it was a lie. I was actually unhappy, sick, and lonely and telling myself my life was full of love, good health, and joy. My subconscious mind did not know it was a lie, though, and I repeated that lie over and over and over until it became truth and the happiness, healthy vitality, and love manifested in reality.

I did not understand what I was doing, but I was becoming an unconscious creator of my life. Instead of responding to whatever happened to come my way, I was shaping the world around me with my thoughts. By gaining control of my mind and thinking only positive and loving thoughts, my life started to be filled with positive and loving things.

As I began to master, love, and improve myself, the world around me was like an answering mirror. I did not know about the universal laws I will discuss later in

Part Three, but I knew there was a definite connection between my thoughts and my results. The more I was able to control my thinking and direct it toward the worthy goals I set for myself, the clearer the path toward the goals became.

My health returned to normal as my mind became clear and I was able to stop filling it with negative and destructive thoughts. I began to experience the peace and happiness I'd been visualizing for so long, and my life took on new meaning. For the first time since arriving in New Zealand, I saw the freedom I had been so fortunate to receive as the greatest gift in the entire world. I decided to embrace the enormous opportunities my new home gave me and began to study with renewed passion and inspiration.

Suddenly, it seemed like there were doors opening all around me. I succeeded in getting a position sterilizing surgical equipment at the local hospital, and I excelled in my studies of English. I made some new friends and began to increase my self-esteem and improve my self-image. I was on my way to achieving the goals I set for myself, and I realized that the hour I spent visualizing my dream life needed to be supplemented by calling on some other great powers I will tell you about in the next chapter.

"The key to your universe is that you can choose." ~Frederick Carl Frieseke

Chapter 16
The Laws

Sir Isaac Newton's law of gravity is exact, inflexible, and unfailing. If you drop an apple from the top of a roof, it will drop down to the ground. It cannot go up. I have come to realize that there are other laws in the universe like Newton's laws of nature. These laws work all the time, and they are inflexible whether you are aware of them or not. Unless you've been hiding under a rock for the last ten years, you've probably heard about the law of attraction. Earl Nightingale explains the great law like this: "If you think in negative terms you will achieve negative results. If you think in positive terms you will achieve positive results."

I used the law of attraction as well as several other universal laws you might not be so familiar with to bring me the peace, happiness, and abundance I now enjoy. Understanding and applying the law of forgiveness, the law of compensation, as well as the law of attraction have enabled me to understand myself better and shifted my perception of the world around me. As Dr. Wayne Dyer so eloquently says, "When you change the way you look at things, the things you look at change." When I changed the way I perceived my world and my surroundings, my surroundings and my world changed for the better.

The law of forgiveness was without question the most difficult law for me to master. I used to believe that forgiveness was to pardon the person who had wronged me, so they could move on with a clean slate. What a grandiose and silly idea! After much contemplation and study on the subject, I realized forgiveness was not necessarily for the benefit of the other person. In most cases, the person you forgive does not even care if you forgive them or not. I forgive others so I can move on with a clean slate.

The act of forgiveness is to let go of something and release it completely. I knew I had to forgive the Angkar, the Khmer Rouge, and the privileged Cambodians who tormented and harassed my family. For me to move on, I had to forgive everybody who wronged us along our journey from our happy life in Phnom Penh to our current life in New Zealand. I had to let go and release the past. Not because the Angkar and the Khmer Rouge cared or asked for my forgiveness but because I wanted to move forward in my life.

Buddha explains how holding on to your anger hurts you when he says: "Holding on to anger is like grasping a hot coal with the intent of throwing it at someone else; you are the one who gets burned." For me to move forward in my life and heal, I had to forgive the past and all those who hurt me.

Do I wish the Khmer Rouge had not murdered almost two million people? Do I wish my father were still alive? Of course I do! To wish otherwise would be foolish. However, the genocide happened, and nothing can change that fact. I had to let it go. I had to forgive and release it completely so I could move on and have a clean slate for my bright future.

Forgiving the genocide and subsequent tumultuous life I led was almost as liberating as when the Vietnamese physically freed us from the camps. I suddenly experienced a feeling of lightness and excitement about the future that I had not felt in many years. For the first time since I was a little girl, I looked to the future with eyes no longer narrowed in fear and suspicion, and it felt wonderful.

I savored my freedom and began to relish in my daily accomplishments. I was making rapid progress, and, unbeknown to me, my superiors noticed my strong work ethic. I did not know the law of compensation by name, but I understood the principle and applied it to my job at the hospital.

The law of compensation says you must do your work to the best of your ability and when you have grown too skilled for your current position, you will draw something larger or better to you. The law also states that you must earn what you receive. I put this law to work and became the first staff member in the hospital to promote myself from the entry-level position sterilizing surgical equipment to the position of anes-thesiologist's technician working in an oper-ating theater, which requires several years of training.

Having survived fourteen-hour work-days during the years under the Khmer Rouge, I was not afraid of hard work. In fact, I was so enthusiastic and grateful for the opportunity to earn my own money that taking breaks seldom occurred to me. I must admit I avoided taking meals in the break room because I was fearful of speaking English with the other workers, but largely, I wanted to be certain I earned every dollar I was paid.

My strong work ethic and positive attitude coupled with the universal laws and principles I invoked soon paid off, and I began my climb to the position I currently enjoy. There were many factors that contributed to my promotion, but I know the law of compensation worked in my favor. I always made sure I gave my best, exceeded my requirements, and worked for the entire duration I was paid for. I knew I had to earn what I received even if I was unable to articulate it at the time.

Though I was busy with my studies and my work, I made time for my morning visualization without exception. I knew the visualization had played a vital part in my physical healing and helped me gain my new lease on life. I also noticed that the more I visualized, the clearer the images became.

Each morning started with me opening the door to my beautiful new home in my mind. I would feel the sharp intake of my breath as I marveled at the beauty of the foyer and felt the overwhelming gratitude that I possessed such a magnificent home. My desire increased with each moment I spent, and I began to invoke the great law of attraction when I coupled my desire with expectancy.

Raymond Holliwell says, "Desire without expectation is idle wishing or dreaming." I was not familiar with Holliwell's fine work at the time, but I know the way to my dream home did not even begin to show itself until I began to expect to own the home and look for ways to make my dream a reality.

My expectant attitude told people I deserved the best, and the best was what I received. I no longer felt inferior to anybody, and my new self-confidence brought me everything I needed to build the home from my dreams.

Making the shift from victim of circumstance to creator of my destiny was simple. It was not easy; it took focus, persistence, and a lot of mental strength, but it was simple. I aligned myself with universal laws and began living my life accordingly, and I also began to live according to the principles I share in the next chapter.

"Gratitude is the healthiest of all human emotions. The more you express gratitude for what you have, the more likely you will have even more to express gratitude for." ~Zig Ziglar

Chapter 17
Gratitude, Faith, and Persistence

In addition to the great laws of the universe, there are principles I use to guide and direct me toward my goals. The principles of gratitude, faith, and persistence played a crucial role in my healing from the pain and grief I suffered after losing my family, my country, and my way of life. I still live by these principles and call upon them when I am faced with one of the challenges that inevitably arise on the road of life. I also use these principles to remind myself of life's blessings and to attract more of what I desire into my life.

The first of these principles is gratitude. I am grateful and exude gratitude in every action and aspect of my life. What am I grateful for? First of all, I am grateful for the opportunity to enjoy life for many more years than my beloved father and almost two million of my countrymen. The very small percentage of newcomers who survived the genocide is extremely lucky and must view each day as a gift from God. It would be easy to dwell on the loss I suffered. My grandma and many others who lost loved ones never moved past their grief and into peace and happiness. By consciously choosing an attitude of gratitude and forgiving the past, I ensure that I remain free from the prison of grief and sorrow.

I am also grateful for every experience in my life. People often misunderstand this and ask how I can possibly be grateful for the tragedy that surrounds Cambodia and look at me as if I've lost my marbles. I explain that I cannot change the past, so I choose to let it go and forgive. I then explain that the gratitude I feel is not for the events themselves but for their influence in shaping and molding me into the person I am today. I am blessed to enjoy excellent health, a loving husband, and two wonderful children. I have a thriving business, a meaningful and fulfilling career, and a wide circle of caring friends and family. My life is full of joy and

serenity, and for these and many other blessings, I am deeply grateful.

My gratitude for my past and present
is just the beginning. I am grateful for the
blessings and experiences not yet manifested.
That's right. I exude gratitude for goals not
yet achieved, relationships not yet formed,
milestones not yet reached and excellent
health not quite achieved. I have faith that
these and all the other blessings I truly desire
are on their way, and I am grateful for them
right now.

By feeling grateful for the blessings
not yet manifested, I align myself with the
second principle I use in my life: Faith.
Belief in the unseen and often unknown has
brought me an abundance of blessings and
much comfort during times of hardship.
From the time I was a very young girl, my
parents taught me to believe and trust in a
power I could not see, hear, smell or touch.
They instilled this belief that carried me
through many troubling times.

I believe that I am the creator of my
experiences and my destiny. I do not have
the power to influence or change the
actions and behavior of others, but I can
choose what to feel and think in every set

of circumstances. My faith in God allows me to believe that everything works out as it should and frees me from the self-doubt and pain I might otherwise experience when I think about the past and how I would have liked it to be. My faith comforts me when I grieve for my father and the experiences he missed by reminding me that his spirit is alive and has returned to God.

Faith in my ability to achieve the goals I set drives me to keep striving and working steadily toward their fulfillment. When I find myself thinking that certain goals are out of reach and that I cannot possibly expect to achieve them, I simply remind myself that God delivers whatever we need to fulfill our worthy ideals right on schedule. It is my job to mix faith with persistence and gratitude.

In Napoleon Hill's timeless masterpiece, *Think and Grow Rich,* Hill says, "There can be no heroic connotation to the word persistence, but the quality is to the character of man what carbon is to steel." Persistence is the character trait that enables a person to keep working toward a goal long after the majority of people would have given up.

When I first decided I would own a home within three years, people told me I was crazy. "You can't do that, Pisey," they said. "You don't even speak English! Who would want to hire you? Where is the money for a house coming from when you can't find a job?" These were the most common questions people asked when I told them about my goal. There were others that were more hurtful, but even the most diplomatic and kind friends and relatives asked these questions.

Truthfully, I did not have the answers to their questions. I did not know how I would achieve my goal, but I knew I would. I kept my goal before me and thought about it every morning when I got up and every night before I went to sleep. No matter how many people told me it could not be done, I did not allow their words to distract me from doing my best at my job and studies.

The focus and hard work paid off. As I continued to persist and work steadily toward my goal, the means by which I was to obtain it began to emerge. I achieved a high grade in my English course and was encouraged to take the test that resulted in my acceptance for training as an anesthesiologist's assistant. Despite the nay-sayers who treated me like a second-class cit-izen, I was determined to earn my position in the operating theater working side-by-side with some of the country's finest doctors.

My determination and belief in myself allowed me to keep working despite the self-doubt I felt. As Earl Nightingale says, "Persistence is simply another word for faith. If you did not have faith, you would never persist."

Faith, persistence, and gratitude kept me motivated and moving toward my goal when it completely defied logic. In the beginning, when my goal seemed completely out of reach and ridiculous, these principles kept me on track and helped me to keep my desires in the forefront of my mind.

My formula for success is based on the principles of gratitude, faith, and persistence coupled with the universal laws of attrac-tion, compensation, and forgiveness. As you will read in the concluding chapter of this book, the 4P method is the hidden seed of advantage.

"The starting point of all achievement is desire." ~Napoleon Hill

Chapter 18
The Seed of Equivalent Advantage

Growing up under the Khmer Rouge and then the communist Vietnamese government was, at best, tremendously difficult. Our escape from Cambodia, where we were chased through the jungle by armed men and narrowly escaped land mines, was terrifying. When we finally arrived at a refugee camp only to be forced to hide in a hole under the ground for a year, it almost broke my spirit.

Almost is the key word. I survived the labor camps and the jungle flights and the night raids and the bandits. I felt empowered by the obstacles I overcame and let them motivate me to find my true greatness.

I experienced a low point when we first arrived in New Zealand because I was overwhelmed by all the freedom I was experiencing for the first time and got stuck in a cycle of negative and destructive thinking. I suspect the ten previous years of fearing for my survival played their toll on my psyche, and I desperately needed some self-love.

I did not know what I did when I invoked the laws of forgiveness, attraction, and compensation into my life. I could not articulate why I spent my mornings visualizing the life I wanted to create. I would not be able to explain the great principles of gratitude, faith, and persistence to somebody who asked. Yet I used these great truths unconsciously, without knowing why or even how I knew to use them, and the reward has been enormous beyond belief.

For about ten years, I was what you would call an unconscious creator. I was very definitely creating my life and molding my world with my thoughts, but I did not understand why this was happening. Then I discovered some great teachers like Napoleon Hill, Robert Kiyosaki, Bob Proctor and Earl Nightingale.

I began to learn about myself and some of the paradigms that were helping me as well as some that were holding me back.

The most influential line I read came from Napoleon Hill's *Think and Grow Rich* when Hill says, "Every failure carries with it the seed of an equivalent advantage." That was the answer to my questions and the explanation for why I was creating such a magical life for myself.

Without actually knowing these words, I'd spent the last ten years looking for seeds of advantage in every tragedy, adversity, failure, upset and loss I experienced. When you realize they each have the seed of an equivalent advantage, you will see that there were many seeds of great advantage to sow.

It was no longer a surprise to me when I achieved my goals and saw my desires manifest. I was living in alignment with universal laws and truths, so the worthy goals had to come into fruition.

Perhaps the greatest seed of advantage is the one I will share with you, my dear reader. This is my personal formula for success. If you decide on a worthy ideal, set a clearly defined goal for yourself, and incorporate my 4P method into your morning, you will be bountifully rewarded for your efforts. The sky is the limit for anyone who can tap into this unlimited source of supply.

Here are the 4 P's I practice every morning.

1. Practice—Meditation and visualization
2. Purpose—Write or read your goals several times
3. Prioritize—Decide what needs to be done that day and order it according to its importance
4. Pay gratitude—Be grateful for what you have already received, and be grateful for the rich bounty that is on its way

It's as marvelous and as simple as that. If you will take the time to decide what you really want, set a goal, and truly commit to the 4P method, you will almost certainly reach your goal.

Meditation and visualization connect you with the source, and as we heard on the Sermon on the Mount, "Ask and it shall be given, seek and ye shall find, knock and it shall be opened unto you." You must be willing to ask the creator for what you desire, and you must be clear and concise in your request.

The purpose of writing and reading your goals multiple times is to plant them firmly in the treasury of your subconscious mind. Then, when you least expect it, you will come up with a brilliant idea that will take you closer to the attainment of your goal and the fulfillment of your purpose.

Prioritizing is crucial in your daily routine because it keeps you focused on what matters. Too often, we get tangled up in daily trivia and lose sight of what matters. It is important to remain balanced during the pursuit of your goal, but it is even more important to stay focused on what matters most.

Paying gratitude is probably the easiest and most important of the 4 P's. Look around you. No matter what your present circumstances are, there is something to be grateful for. It might only be that you have eyes with which to read this book and a mind that can comprehend the awesome message it conveys. Or you might be a billionaire looking to reconnect with yourself. No matter who you are, regardless of your circumstances, there is always something to be grateful for. An attitude of gratitude both for the things you already have and for the things that have yet to manifest is guaranteed to bring you closer to your goal.

So what is the seed of equivalent advantage from growing up under the Khmer Rouge? It is celebration. Celebration because it should make you realize that if I can succeed beyond my wildest fantasies, then so can you. I was tortured, starved, enslaved, hunted, harassed, set free and have turned my once miserable life spent entirely as a victim into a life where I am the undisputed master of my destiny and the creator of my dreams.

You can do this, too! Decide now to grab hold of your dreams, set your goal, and begin to use the 4P method. You will change your life, and in the process, you will inspire countless others.

See you at the top!

About the Author

Pisey Leng has a truly incredible and uplifting story to tell. She is a survivor of the infamous killing fields of Cambodia that in the late 70's claimed the lives of almost two million innocent people. Among them were Pisey's father, grandparents, aunts, uncles and cousins.

Although she was living in fear within a world of unspeakable horror, a light shined within Pisey that kept her determined to survive.

After living inside a brutal four-year ordeal under the murderous Khmer Rouge, Pisey and her mother and brother did everything they could to build a new life under the communist Vietnamese government.

Ultimately, it was her brother's conscription that sparked her family's harrowing escape from Cambodia to a refugee camp in Thailand.

After more than a year of dealing with the daily challenges that come with living as an illegal refugee, and three more tense years waiting for a country to accept them—Pisey and her family finally were able to move to New Zealand.

Pisey arrived in her new country carrying all of her life possessions in a flimsy cardboard box. She immediately faced a new set of obstacles, including the many that came from her inability to speak English.

However, after all she had been through, Pisey made a conscious decision to stand tall and move forward with courage and determination. And though it wasn't easy, she did so with incredible grace.

Within 10 years Pisey established herself in a distinguished career as an anesthesiologist's technician. She also owns a thriving bakery, is a proud Vemma representative and has amassed considerable wealth through real estate investing.

A truly amazing turnaround in a life that had witnessed so much tragedy.

Pisey has devoted her life to her family, her career and studying the world's most respected personal development leaders. She credits the teaching of Napolean Hill, Bob Proctor and Robert Kiyosaki with helping her develop the 4P method she uses to maximize her potential.

Today, Pisey is a beacon of inspiration to those who face any life challenge, no matter how severe. She is deeply committed to helping others learn how to find the seed of advantage in any adversity, so they too can enjoy a life of peace, happiness and abundance.

http://PiseyL.vemma.com

CPSIA information can be obtained at www.ICGtesting.com
Printed in the USA
LVOW07s1602200515

439230LV00001B/68/P

9 780992 011635